The Travails of Two Woodpeckers

THE TRAVAILS OF
TWO WOODPECKERS

IVORY-BILLS & IMPERIALS

NOEL F. R. SNYDER :: DAVID E. BROWN :: KEVIN B. CLARK

UNIVERSITY OF NEW MEXICO PRESS :: ALBUQUERQUE

Library of Congress Cataloging-in-Publication Data

Snyder, Noel F. R.

The travails of two woodpeckers : ivory-bills and imperials / Noel F.R. Snyder, David E. Brown, Kevin B. Clark.

   p.   cm.

Includes bibliographical references and index.

ISBN 978-0-8263-4664-3 (alk. paper)

1. Ivory-billed woodpecker. 2. Imperial woodpecker. 3. Rare birds— Conservation. I. Brown, David E. (David Earl), 1938– II. Clark, Kevin B., 1971– III. Title.

QL696.P56S694 2009

   598.7'2—dc22

2009001013

Book design and type composition by Melissa Tandysh

Composed in 10.15/14 ScalaOT

Display type is Caxton Std Book and Poetica Std

To the historical figures who provided the most crucial
information on the biology and plight of ivory-bills and imperials:

Alexander Wilson

John James Audubon

Edwin Hasbrouck

Arthur Wayne

Carl Lumholtz

Edward Nelson

Arthur Allen

James Tanner

Herbert Stoddard

John Dennis

George Lamb

Walter Bishop

Minor McGlaughlin

CONTENTS

LIST OF ILLUSTRATIONS

MAPS

ACKNOWLEDGMENTS

The contributions of the late James Tanner to our present understanding of the biology of both imperial and ivory-billed woodpeckers cannot be overstated and loom in the background of all contemporary publications on these species. No comprehensive analysis of these species can be conducted without consulting Tanner's 1940, 1941, 1942, and 1964 publications, as well as his detailed field notes and correspondence on file at Cornell University. These materials constitute a tremendous resource still not fully evaluated by anyone and remain the most important key to understanding these species, whatever hypothesis may be under consideration. Thus, even though we question several of Tanner's conclusions in this book, there is no choice but to rely heavily on Tanner's own data in investigating alternatives.

We further emphasize that the conservation recommendations we favor for these species do not differ in any substantial degree from the recommendations put forth by Tanner, and we do not in any way fault Tanner for the apparent ultimate failure of conservation efforts for these species. Tanner clearly recognized that human depredations were a severe threat that had to be dealt with effectively if these two species were to survive but, sadly, his recommendations on this subject continue to be undervalued today, just as his recommendations for habitat conservation were never comprehensively implemented.

With respect to ivory-bill matters in particular, we also wish to acknowledge the pivotal importance of the late Minor McGlaughlin of Okeechobee County, Florida, whose early observations on local ivory-bills provided a major stimulus to delve into the historical literature on ivory-bills and led ultimately to the development of many of the ideas presented in this book. Also very important in stimulating this process have been the excellent recent books by Christopher Cokinos (2000), Jerry Jackson (2004), Philip Hoose (2004), Tim Gallagher (2005), and Geoff Hill (2007). We gratefully acknowledge a personal debt to these people who have preceded us in addressing many of the matters considered here, and whose own historical research efforts and insights have revealed many important facets of the biology of these species. Much of what we present here on ivory-bills was excerpted from the senior author's (NFRS) more detailed monograph on the species published by the Western Foundation of Vertebrate Zoology in 2007.

For critical comments on various drafts of ivory-bill materials we also wish to express our special thanks to Steve Beissinger, Alan Craig, Rod Drewein, Linnea Hall, Jerry Jackson, Martjan Lammertink, Bill Mannan, Allan Mee, Vicky Meretsky, Narca Moore-Craig, Ian Newton, Peter Warshall, Jim Wiley, and Joe Wunderle. Jim Wiley was especially helpful in supplying much important background material on Cuban ivory-bills and their interactions with rural human populations and in providing access to the historical correspondence of Charles Ramsden. Will Post of the Charleston Museum and Mary LeCroy of the American Museum of Natural History made available the early correspondence of Arthur Wayne, Frank Chapman, and J. A. Allen. The Museum of Comparative Zoology at Harvard granted access to the additional correspondence of Arthur Wayne and William Brewster. Vicky Meretsky was very helpful in analyzing various quantitative matters discussed in the book. Wylie Barrow and Heather Baldwin graciously shared interview information they had obtained on historical matters pertaining to the Singer Tract, while Nancy Tanner (the wife of James Tanner) and George and Nancy Lamb kindly provided additional insights regarding their personal knowledge of historical ivory-bill studies.

For the location and use of various photographs relevant to ivory-bill matters, we are indebted to Jim Wiley, Ron Austing, Richard Sevier, Eleanor Rawlings, Nancy Tanner, George Lamb, the Tall Timbers Research Station, the Cornell Laboratory of Ornithology, the Charleston Museum, the New York Historical Society, and the American Philosophical Society. Narca Moore-Craig kindly created the color plate of ivory-bills, and Richard Wagner aided in the restoration of historical photographs.

With respect to imperial woodpecker assistance, we are especially indebted to Dr. William Hankins of La Sierra University and Mr. Walter Bishop of Durango, Mexico, for sharing personal observations and recollections of imperial woodpeckers decades ago. We also thank Bob Howard for allowing us to photograph his pair of mounted imperial woodpeckers from Chihuahua, Mexico. Dr. David Pearson of the School of Life Sciences at Arizona State University prepared the distribution maps and put us in touch with entomologist Frank Hovore in Santa Clarita,

California. Sandy Lanham of Environmental Flying Services in Tucson, Arizona, piloted us over the Sierra Madre Occidental, and Dana Fisher of the Ernst Mayr Library at MCZ tracked down important correspondence from W. W. Brown. Both Dr. Raul Valdez of New Mexico State University at Las Cruces and Gale Monson of Oro Valley, Arizona, provided us with obscure but important publications referencing imperial woodpeckers. We would especially like to thank Randall Babb, Bill Broyles, Neil Carmony, Javier Díaz, Rod Dossey, Bruce Duke, Jill Bielowski, Richard D. Fisher, Rich Glinski, Terry Johnson, Carlos Lopez González, Mike Perkinson, John Phelps, Frank Reichenbacher, Mike Robinson, Barry Spicer, and Jean and Ray Turner for sharing our rewards and discomforts on various trips to the Sierra Madre and its environs. Their company made each trip a delight. Ron Cole, formerly at the University of California at Davis, was especially helpful in contacting the curators of the various museums with ornithological collections. In this regard we would especially like to thank Ellen Alers, assistant archivist with the SI; Kelli Anderson, AMNH research librarian; Carol Ann Beardmore, USFWS; Sara Ann Biggs, Kingman Museum in Battle Creek, MI; Fritz Hertel, UCLA; Brad Miller, Royal Ontario Museum; James R. Northern, Moore Laboratory of Zoology at Occidental College in Los Angeles, CA; Stephanie Ogeneski, National Anthropological Archives, Smithsonian Institution; Lloyd Kiff, Western Foundation of Vertebrate Zoology, Camarillo, CA; Robin K. Panza, Carnegie Museum of Natural History; Jim Patton, MVZ; José (Pepe) Treviño; Cynthia E. Rebar, Edinboro University of Pennsylvania; Linda Simeone, Natural History Museum of Los Angeles County; Tice Supplee, Sonora Chapter of the Audubon Society; Robert Prys-Jones of the Natural History Museum, London; and all of the other curators who made a special attempt to satisfy our too many requests.

We would also like to express our special appreciation to William Calder, Sam Campana, Guillermo Carrillo, Nigel Collar, Alejandro Espinosa, Bill Huey, Carlos Galindo Leal, Gale Monson, Dean Hendrickson, Jerry Jackson, Martjan Lammertink, Bonnie Swarbrick, Roberto Uranga, David Wege, and Dr. Joe Wilder for providing us both valuable insights and contributing especially useful assistance.

This book is based on papers originally delivered in abbreviated form at the Special Symposium on the Ecology of Large Woodpeckers held in Brinkley, Arkansas, from October 31 to November 3, 2005, and also relies heavily on materials presented in Snyder (2007).

INTRODUCTION

The central reaches of North America once hosted two of the most spectacular woodpeckers in the world—the enormous imperial woodpecker (*Campephilus imperialis*), a native of the pine forests of the Sierra Madre Occidental of Mexico, and the closely related but somewhat smaller ivory-billed woodpecker (*Campephilus principalis*), a resident of the bottomland swamp forests of the southeastern United States, but also found in pine and hardwood forests of Cuba. Early naturalists described both species as quite common in pristine woodlands, but both were known to be in serious decline toward the end of the nineteenth century. Today both are either extinct or sufficiently rare and elusive that there have been no conclusive records of their existence in recent decades. Tantalizing reports of sightings continue, but all may be based on misidentifications of other similar species. No recent sightings have been convincingly replicated or fully confirmed by unassailable hard evidence, and all as yet have failed to achieve universal acceptance.

In life, both woodpeckers were nearly 2 feet long, and indeed the imperial was the largest woodpecker known for the entire planet. The ivory-bill ranked third in size behind the imperial and the great slaty woodpecker (*Mulleripicus pulverulentus*) of Borneo and Malaysia. Both ivory-bills and imperials were largely black in plumage, but both also possessed expansive white wing patches on the flight feathers close to the body—feathers known technically as secondaries. At rest, these patches gave a conspicuous white coloration to the terminal portions of the folded wings, and in flight they gave a wide white edge to trailing portions of the wings. The large size of individuals and the white secondary patches have long been considered the most important visual characteristics for identifying both species under natural conditions.

Other important field marks of these species included two parallel white feather stripes running from the white secondary patches up the back. In the ivory-bill these stripes continued on up the neck and cheeks of the birds almost to the eyes, but in the imperial the neck and cheeks were solid black. Males of both species displayed brilliant red crests with black leading edges, while females had totally black crests. The crest in female imperial woodpeckers was very distinctive in shape, recurving up, around, and forward toward the bill, presenting a most unusual outline to the head in profile—quite different from the more disheveled crest of female ivory-bills. Both the imperial woodpecker and the ivory-billed woodpecker also had conspicuous lemon-yellow eyes and massive ivory-colored bills.

The ivory-bill persisted long enough in one virgin forest of northeastern Louisiana—the Singer Tract—to permit a thorough ecological study by James Tanner in the late 1930s. In pursuing his PhD at Cornell University, Tanner spent parts of four breeding seasons recording all he could on the behavior of some of the last living individuals, and during the fall and winter seasons he attempted to find additional individuals in other remnant virgin forests elsewhere in the southeastern states. In his monograph on the species, Tanner (1942) concluded that only about two dozen ivory-bills still existed in the United States and that prospects for survival of the species were grim primarily because of logging but also because of shooting.

Persuasive reports of the ivory-bill have been relatively few in the United States since the time of Tanner's study, but have had a wide geographic distribution. The last fully accepted sighting in the Singer Tract was in 1944, but Whitney Eastman (1958) presented reasonably credible evidence of a few individuals persisting along the Chipola River of Florida in 1950 and 1951, and John Dennis (1967) reported sightings and sound-recording evidence of a few individuals in the Big Thicket region of Texas in the late 1960s. Among other more recent and more controversial sightings perhaps the most notable have been individuals reported along the

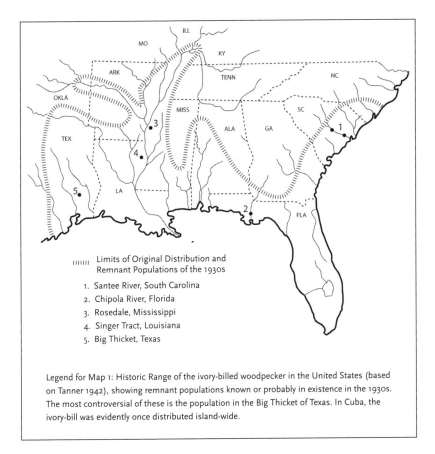

IIIIIII Limits of Original Distribution and
Remnant Populations of the 1930s

1. Santee River, South Carolina
2. Chipola River, Florida
3. Rosedale, Mississippi
4. Singer Tract, Louisiana
5. Big Thicket, Texas

Legend for Map 1: Historic Range of the ivory-billed woodpecker in the United States (based on Tanner 1942), showing remnant populations known or probably in existence in the 1930s. The most controversial of these is the population in the Big Thicket of Texas. In Cuba, the ivory-bill was evidently once distributed island-wide.

MAP 1.
Historical distribution of the ivory-billed woodpecker in the southeastern United States.

Achafalaya River in Louisiana in the early 1970s (Lowery 1974), and in eastern Arkansas and northern Florida in the mid-2000s (Fitzpatrick et al. 2005; Hill et al. 2006). Sporadic searches for the species continue in many parts of its original range in the southeastern states, despite the absence of any fully confirmed sightings in recent decades (map 1). These searches have been especially intensive and extensive since reports of the species in Arkansas were announced in 2005.

Meanwhile, John Dennis (1948) found three individuals of a remnant ivory-bill population in cutover pine forest of eastern Cuba and obtained clear photographs of the species at an active nest. Then in 1956 George

Lamb and his wife Nancy conducted a single-season study (1957) documenting thirteen individuals in this same population. Additional credible sightings of individuals in this population were reported as recently as the late 1980s (Short and Horne 1986, 1987; Lammertink and Estrada 1995; Jackson 2004), and rumors are still heard that the species may persist elsewhere in Cuba.

The imperial woodpecker was never studied thoroughly by any ornithologist or ecologist, and many aspects of its natural history remain obscure. No sound recordings of a living bird are known to exist, no nests were ever closely observed, and no eggs of the species can be found in museums. Field information on the biology of the imperial is limited largely to a brief summary by E. W. Nelson (1898) of a short trip in 1892 during which he observed twenty to twenty-two imperials in Michoacán, and to scattered reports, mostly associated with specimen collecting in various other parts of its original range, which extended north in the Sierra Madre Occidental to just shy of the U.S. border in Chihuahua and Sonora (map 2). One of the last credible sightings was obtained in 1946 by Arthur A. Allen (1951) in Durango. This was followed by other credible sightings in Durango by William L. Rhein, a U.S. dentist, in 1954 and 1956. One of Rhein's sightings was substantiated by good-quality motion picture footage now archived at Cornell University's Laboratory of Ornithology, the only photographic evidence of a living imperial ever obtained.

James Tanner (1964) made still another expedition to search for the species in Durango in 1962, but failed to find any birds, although he obtained very recent reports of imperials from local residents. Other mid- to late twentieth-century searches, including those of Fleming and Baker (1963), Plimpton (1977), Gallina (1981), E. A. Hankins (pers. comm. 2005), and W. C. Bishop (pers. comm. 2004), likewise failed to produce sightings of living imperials. Perhaps the most ambitious of the recent efforts, but similarly fruitless, have been those of Uranga-Thomas and Venegas-Holguin (1995), Lammertink et al. (1996), and ourselves (DEB and KBC)—our own efforts extending intermittently from 1970 to 2002.

Nevertheless, as detailed especially in Lammertink et al. (1996), seemingly credible reports of imperial woodpeckers stemming from other sources have continued throughout the twentieth century, and current persistence of the species, while doubtful, is not to be ruled out completely. The original range of the imperial was large (nearly 1,000 miles long and 100 miles wide), and no comprehensive search of all regions

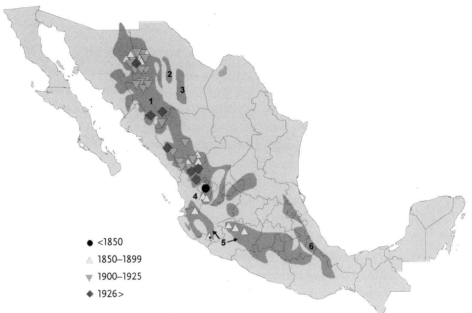

● <1850
△ 1850–1899
▽ 1900–1925
◆ 1926>

Map 2. Imperial Woodpecker specimen locations.

Principal Conifer Forests
1. Sierra Madre Occidental
2. Sierra Catarina
3. Sierra del Nido
4. Sierra Los Bolaños
5. Transvolcanic Ranges
6. Sierra Madre Oriental

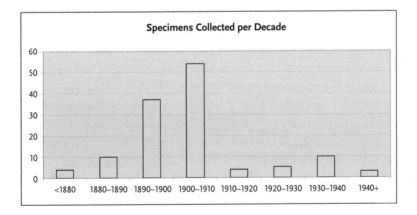

MAP 2.

Historical distribution of the imperial woodpecker (symbols) and the progression of collected specimens.

remaining under forest cover has yet been conducted (map 2). Such an effort would be a truly formidable undertaking.

The ivory-billed woodpecker recently received a tremendous amount of international publicity when its rediscovery in the bottomland swamps of eastern Arkansas was announced in early 2005 by a group of observers based at Cornell University's Laboratory of Ornithology (Fitzpatrick et al. 2005). This announcement was supported by a series of brief visual sightings and a video of marginal quality that have since been questioned by several parties (Jackson 2006; Sibley et al. 2006; Collinson 2007). Unfortunately, convincing subsequent confirmation of the ivory-bill's existence in Arkansas has not been forthcoming, despite massive field efforts (Stokstad 2007). In like manner, recent reported sightings of this species in swamps along the Chocktawhatchee River of Florida have yet to be followed with fully persuasive confirming evidence (Hill et al. 2006).

In both Arkansas and Florida, potential sightings of ivory-bills have to be very carefully discriminated from sightings of the visually similar pileated woodpecker (*Dryocopus pileatus*). And although the pileated is a smaller species, it is only slightly smaller and is also a largely black woodpecker with considerable white visible on its wings in flight. In brief and distant sightings it can easily be mistaken for the ivory-bill. This is especially true for the occasional odd pileated possessing white secondaries. In 1979, one of us (NFRS) had a detailed close observation of such an aberrant pileated in central Florida, a bird that might easily have been reported as an ivory-bill had it only been seen flying by at a long distance (see Snyder and Snyder 2006: 125–26).

Sightings of the imperial woodpecker also pose potential difficulties with mistaken identities, even though this species did not share its historical high-elevation range with any other species of large woodpecker. Lowland regions adjacent to much of the imperial's original range still host two other large black-and-white woodpeckers—the lineated woodpecker (*Dryocopus lineatus*) and the pale-billed woodpecker (*Campephilus guatemalensis*). Thus, the possibility exists that occasional individuals of these latter two species may wander up into the former range of the imperial and be misidentified as that species. Indeed, the local Mexican name of the imperial woodpecker—*pitoreál*—is sometimes applied as well to the pale-billed woodpecker.

Only the range of the ivory-billed woodpecker in Cuba is completely isolated from the distributions of other large black-and-white woodpeckers, and only on this island are the chances of confusing ivory-bills with other large woodpeckers effectively absent. The Cuban crow (*Corvus nasicus*) is similar in size and could be confused with the ivory-bill under poor lighting, but it normally lacks any white feathers and perches and vocalizes very differently.

As engrossing as recent efforts to search for still-extant populations of ivory-bills and imperials have been, it is not our intent to focus closely on these matters in this book. Nor is it our intent to provide a general overview of the biology of these species. Landmark accounts of the behavior, ecology, and history of these species have already been provided by Nelson (1898), Tanner (1942, 1964), Cokinos (2000), Hoose (2004), and Jackson (2002, 2004). For varied and exciting accounts of searches for remnant populations we recommend that the reader consult Plimpton (1977), Lammertink and Estrada (1995), Uranga-Thomas and Venegas-Holguin (1995), Lammertink et al. (1996), Jackson (2004), Hoose (2004), Gallagher (2005), Hill (2007), and Steinberg (2008).

Our goal, instead, is to present a reexamination of the causes of the historical decline of both species and to discuss the conservation implications of these causes. Our views on these subjects differ in important respects from widespread contemporary views, and we believe that future conservation prospects of these and other species can benefit from a detailed look at alternative explanations and strategies.

In most accounts, both the ivory-bill and the imperial have been viewed as victims of relentless and thorough lumbering of their original habitats, and indeed their declines appeared to roughly parallel the cutting of the original forests of the continent. Yet habitat destruction, as the major agent of decline, has difficulty accounting for the disappearance of these species from some substantial regions before concerted lumbering began. Evidently, populations in these locations had already been strongly reduced or obliterated by factors other than timber harvest. Also posing some difficulties for the habitat-destruction hypothesis is the long persistence of the last fully confirmed ivory-bill population in Cuba, which for nearly a half century occupied a region that had been devastated by logging.

An alternative explanation for the demise of these woodpeckers is widespread and relentless depredations, both by indigenous Native Americans and by early settlers and their descendants from other continents.

Both woodpeckers were large enough, tasty enough, noisy enough, and approachable enough to be frequent targets for subsistence hunters. When birds collected for scientific specimens, display mounts, and bill trophies are added to the mix, not to mention killings for curiosity and sport, these species may simply have been too desirable and vulnerable to have had any appreciable chances for long-term coexistence with our own species.

Clearly, both human depredations and habitat destruction occurred during the declines of these woodpeckers, and these stresses should not be considered mutually exclusive. Moreover, these are not the only negative factors that may have affected these species. Nevertheless, as we will develop in the chapters ahead, it appears probable that human depredations were the primary factor in the difficulties of both species, and that while habitat destruction was also important, it was a lesser factor, and may well have contributed to the species' declines mainly by facilitating human depredations, rather than by diminishing food supplies. In general, lumbering provides greatly increased access to formerly remote forested regions and greatly swells the numbers of people frequenting these forests—effects that greatly increase the risks of depredations for vulnerable species. In importance, these effects can easily overshadow any declines in food supplies produced by the same timbering activities, especially when timbering is only selective and leaves many food-rich snags and defective trees standing.

Emphasizing depredations is not a new point of view, but one largely forgotten since the ivory-bill studies of Tanner (1942), who believed that lumbering's negative effects on food supplies were the major cause of that species' decline. Tanner's conclusions soon achieved center stage in the thinking of most conservationists and have remained conventional wisdom to this day. Yet much of the early lumbering of ivory-bill habitats involved only selective cutting of trees, and early accounts of the ivory-bill are silent about potential food scarcity for the species. Tanner's own studies appear to indicate normal reproductive effort and success in the declining remnant population he studied—something one might not expect in a food-stressed population.

At the same time, nearly all early accounts of both species recorded shooting or other human depredations, and many early observers, including such luminaries as John James Audubon, emphasized the vulnerability of these species because of their approachability and characteristically steady and distinctive vocalizations. Compared with many other species of birds and mammals, these woodpeckers were evidently ill-prepared to survive well-armed humanity because of their fairly large size, conspicuous and relatively unwary habits, and modest reproductive rates. And while the last individuals in many populations were noticeably more wary than the norm, time was evidently too short for them to evolve truly effective protection against the capacities of our own species to destroy them. Loss of these species may have been inevitable in the absence of concerted and effective efforts to protect them from depredations.

This book had its origins at the Large Woodpecker Symposium held in Brinkley, Arkansas, in late 2005. At that meeting the three of us presented papers on the declines of the ivory-billed and imperial woodpeckers and discovered that our conclusions regarding causes of endangerment were so similar, yet so different from conventional wisdom, that it seemed worthwhile to bring together the available information for both species in a single book focused specifically on their common problems and conservation needs. The book that has emerged here considers first the history of decline and causes of extinction of the ivory-billed woodpecker in a chapter by NFRS that highlights and updates materials in his recently published monograph on the species for the Western Foundation of Vertebrate Zoology (Snyder 2007). The ivory-bill chapter is followed by a chapter by DEB and KBC that considers the decline of the imperial woodpecker and represents an expansion of their presentation at the Arkansas conference. In a final chapter and epilogue we combine forces and take a more general viewpoint of the two species, considering a variety of matters, especially some general conservation insights to be gleaned from their tragic histories.

Both here and in Snyder (2007), the ivory-billed woodpecker is considered to have two primary populations, one in the southeastern United States (subspecies *principalis*) and one in Cuba (subspecies *bairdi*), although we point out that recent genetic research has led to a recommendation to raise these two subspecies to full species rank, despite the close similarity in body size and visual characteristics of the two populations (Fleischer et al. 2006). Regardless of whether one favors recognition of one ivory-bill species or two, it is important to examine both populations traditionally considered to be ivory-billed woodpeckers for the comparative insights they can provide as to causes of endangerment.

The imperial woodpecker, so far as is known, never had any separate island populations and has never been subdivided into subspecies, although it has sometimes been recognized as constituting a superspecies with the ivory-bill (Mayr and Short 1970). Unfortunately, relatively little biological information is available to evaluate characteristics of the imperial, as it never received detailed study comparable to Tanner's efforts with the ivory-bill. Nevertheless, our chapter on the imperial does include a substantial amount of previously unpublished material dug out of obscure sources such as old government field reports and specimen labels. The new material significantly expands knowledge of such matters as feeding habits and the early status of the species in specific regions.

Our approach with both species is primarily a review of historical sources, including both published reports and unpublished letters and notes of some of the prominent naturalists familiar with the species. In addition we report on personal interviews we have had with individuals familiar with these species in bygone times. But even though we have spent a considerable amount of time in the ranges of these species conducting research on other bird species, none of us has ever encountered a living ivory-bill or living imperial woodpecker. Thus, our analyses here are necessarily based largely on second-hand information, some of which may never be fully validated.

We would much prefer to be reporting conclusions based on our personal observations on these species, as the chances for going astray with misinterpretations are always increased with distance from primary observations. Nevertheless, a focus on second-hand information now appears to be unavoidable and is the difficulty faced by most historians. We struggle onward, relying on the basic assumption that most early naturalists reporting observations of these species were probably not liars and frauds. Thus, when the same assertions were widely and apparently independently offered by many individuals, we tend to give credence to these assertions.

The journey through early historical writings on these species has been a fascinating voyage of discovery in which we have encountered many unanticipated facts and assertions. Our respect for many early naturalists has grown substantially as we have studied their original accounts, and we have been surprised to discover how often these accounts have been distorted, dismissed, or simply ignored without cogent justification in subsequent writings. Surely, some mistakes in interpretation are to be expected in all eras, but valuable insights of those long gone are sometimes forgotten simply because modern writers often assume that secondary accounts are complete and accurate, and fail to examine original sources. We hope that this book contributes to a better balance in evaluating the contributions of our forebears.

Despite a few successes in conserving endangered species, such as the rescue of the whooping crane (*Grus americana*) and trumpeter swan (*Cygnus buccinator*) from excessive subsistence shooting and rescue of the snowy and great egrets (*Egretta thula* and *Ardea alba*) from the inroads of the plume trade, humanity's record so far in ensuring the survival of threatened species has been decidedly mixed, with a growing list of extirpations and extinctions, relatively few examples of full recovery, and many more examples of species hanging on in an uncertain limbo, neither recovered nor extinct. A concern for endangered species is relatively new in the history of our species, and one of the first endangered birds to receive intensive conservation attention was the ivory-bill in the 1930s. Unfortunately, the attention given this species did not come soon enough and was not comprehensive enough to ensure its recovery, despite James Tanner's valiant efforts to mobilize actions on behalf of the species. At the time Tanner's monumental studies were published, the concerns of the nation were thoroughly focused on all-out participation in World War II, so it is perhaps no surprise that needs of the ivory-bill were largely ignored. Indeed, the final lumbering of the Singer Tract in Louisiana and most other virgin bottomland forests of the United States was viewed by many as a policy of patriotism in serving the war effort, despite its negative effects on the ivory-bill. Cokinos (2000), Jackson (2004), and Hoose (2004) give particularly good accounts of the failed efforts of conservationists to stop the lumbering of the Singer Tract.

Concern for the fate of the imperial woodpecker came even later, and by the time researchers began to make serious efforts to refind this species in the late 1940s, 1950s, and 1960s, no one was able to locate more than occasional scattered individuals that most likely did not represent recoverable populations. Nevertheless, nothing like the recent efforts to find remnant populations of the ivory-bill in the United States has ever been mounted on behalf of the imperial.

Both the ivory-bill and the imperial were relatively large and conspicuous birds, both visually and aurally, and, as such, they were not easily missed by rural residents inhabiting their ranges. That both species lasted as long as they did may relate mainly to early limitations in the abilities of humans to kill them, owing to primitive weapons, and to the fact that the primary habitats of these species were among the last to be occupied at any significant densities by our own species.

Human populations have now come to dominate nearly all terrestrial habitats on the planet, and contemporary firearms leave little security for any wildlife species large enough to be eaten. For those species that have the most vulnerability to human influences, the future is uncertain at best. Species that are large, tame, conspicuous, and edible have had a particularly difficult time, and perhaps the surprise is that a few of these species still persist for the moment, although many persist only as zoo populations or as remnants in thoroughly protected wild reserves that owe their continued existence to reasonable levels of political stability in the countries involved. In the long run, neither of these means of protecting species promises a high degree of success, if only because of the long history of instability in human institutions and societies.

The sad tales of the imperial and ivory-billed woodpeckers provide a variety of insights regarding the discouraging process of attempting to conserve charismatic endangered species in the face of steadily growing human populations preoccupied with many other concerns. In reviewing the histories of these species we include some discussion of ways in which research and conservation efforts might have followed a different and more successful path than what actually transpired. We wish there might still be some way to directly test if different strategies might have yielded better results with these species, but that opportunity may now be gone. Nevertheless, we believe it is well worth considering such matters, as these two species are hardly the last species that may disappear in our lifetimes, and many other species face similar problems. Any improvements in general conservation strategies that can be developed to minimize such losses in the future should be encouraged both for practical and aesthetic reasons.

The biosphere did not collapse with the disappearance of the ivory-billed and imperial woodpeckers, but the potentially complete loss of these exceptionally charismatic birds is a major tragedy and a warning of much greater losses of biodiversity ahead. Unless present trends in human population growth and environmental impacts moderate rapidly, future generations may face a world robbed of many of its most valued biotic resources and stressed by truly fundamental threats to its basic life-support systems.

Chapter One

'LAST OF THE IVORY-BILLS

The Sad Decline of a Woodland Spirit

NOEL F. R. SNYDER

I wish, kind reader, it were in my power to present to your mind's eye the favorite resort of the Ivory-billed Woodpecker. Would that I could describe the extent of those deep morasses, overshadowed by millions of gigantic dark cypresses, spreading their sturdy moss-covered branches, as if to admonish intruding man to pause and reflect on the many difficulties which he must encounter, should he persist in venturing farther into their almost inaccessible recesses, extending for miles before him, where he should be interrupted by huge projecting branches, here and there the mossy trunk of a fallen and decaying tree, and thousands of creeping and twining plants of numberless species! Would that I could represent to you the dangerous nature of the ground, its oozing, spongy, and miry disposition, although covered with a beautiful but treacherous carpeting, composed of the richest mosses, flags, and water-lilies, no sooner receiving the pressure of the foot than it yields and endangers the very life of the adventurer, whilst here and there, as he approaches an opening, that proves merely a lake of black muddy water, his ear is assailed by the dismal croaking of innumerable frogs, the hissing of serpents, or the bellowing of alligators!

JOHN JAMES AUDUBON, *Birds of America*, 1842: 21

As had Alexander Wilson before him, Audubon left no ambiguities about the sort of habitat most favored by the ivory-billed woodpecker

(*Campephilus principalis*) in the United States. Occupying lowland swamp forests of the Southeast, but also occurring in a variety of forests in Cuba, the ivory-bill was one of the most charismatic birds in our original avifauna (plate 1). Audubon called it "Vandyke" because of its strikingly handsome appearance and, in his *American ornithology* of 1811, Wilson devoted many fascinating pages to his experiences with it. Here clearly was a species that was as impressive to early ornithologists as were its pristine woodland surroundings.

Neither for Audubon, nor for Wilson, was the ivory-bill a species in obvious jeopardy. Yet in 1891 Edwin Hasbrouck published a long article discussing the declining fortunes of the species and, by 1930, more than three decades before there was a federal Endangered Species Act or any other comprehensive protection for vanishing species, the ivory-bill was considered likely extinct by most ornithologists. The species had not been reliably reported since 1924, when a potential "last pair" was found and briefly studied in central Florida by Arthur Allen of Cornell University. Unfortunately, this pair was soon killed by local taxidermists, and no one in the professional ornithological establishment was then aware of other extant pairs.

Nevertheless, evidence was to emerge within a few years that other remnant populations of the species still existed in parts of South Carolina, Florida, Louisiana, Mississippi, and Cuba (see Allen and Sprunt 1936; Eastman 1958; Pearson 1932; Jackson 2004; Dennis 1948; plate 2). One of these—a population in the 120-square-mile Singer Tract of northeastern Louisiana—was officially "rediscovered" in 1932 through the completely legal collection of a specimen by Mason Spencer, a colorful Louisiana attorney and state legislator who had maintained a hunting camp in the tract for a number of years (fig. 1). Spencer collected this specimen as a deliberate gesture to refute the officials who had ridiculed his claims that the ivory-bill still existed (see Cokinos 2000 and Jackson 2004 for details). This rediscovery led first to a 1935 expedition organized by Arthur A. Allen that made brief observations of the Singer Tract birds (fig. 2), followed by the establishment of a research program financed by the National Audubon Society and carried out by a doctoral student—James Tanner (fig. 3)—who was supervised by Allen at Cornell University (see Tanner 1940, 1941, 1942).

Tanner spent parts of four breeding seasons in intensive field research on the ivory-bill in the late 1930s, and in 1942 he produced the

FIGURE 1.

Mason Spencer (1892–1962), an attorney, hunter, and member of the Louisiana State Legislature, earned an enduring place in history by his 1932 "rediscovery" of the ivory-billed woodpecker in the Singer Tract of the northeastern corner of the state. In this 1936 photograph, he is seen in the tract with Governor Richard Leche and an unidentified gentleman. Spencer attributed the disappearance of the ivory-bill to gunfire.

— PHOTO COURTESY OF MR. RICHARD SEVIER.

only detailed monograph ever put together on first-hand study of the species in nature. His field notes give testimony to the extreme difficulty and considerable risks entailed in following and studying ivory-bills, yet he was ultimately successful in achieving a broad documentation of the species' biology and in developing a comprehensive plan for its conservation. Unfortunately, few of Tanner's conservation recommendations were ever implemented, in part because there was as yet little concern for endangered species within the range of the ivory-bill. Still, in retrospect, much of today's concern for endangered wildlife can be traced to early studies such as Tanner's ivory-bill research and Carl Koford's (1953) research on the California condor (*Gymnogyps californianus*).

Tanner found evidence for an ivory-bill population of seven pairs and four fledglings in the Singer Tract in 1934, but this population steadily declined through the period of his studies, and by 1939 only one pair, one fledgling, and three unpaired males remained. By that time, logging of the Singer Tract was underway, and despite last-ditch efforts of conservationists to halt the cutting, it continued unabated. Further sightings of ivory-bills in the tract declined to zero within a few years. Other remnant populations in South Carolina, Mississippi, and Florida that were not

FIGURE 2.

Arthur A. Allen (1885–1964) was the principal organizer of efforts to observe nesting ivory-billed woodpeckers in the Singer Tract of Louisiana in 1935. Allen was also James Tanner's supervising professor at Cornell University and arranged for the National Audubon Society to provide the support needed for Tanner to carry out subsequent ivory-bill studies. In 1924 Allen had earlier observed a nesting pair of the species in Florida, but those observations were cut short by collection of the birds involved by taxidermists.

—PHOTO BY ARTHUR A. ALLEN, COURTESY OF MACAULAY LIBRARY
AT THE CORNELL LAB OF ORNITHOLOGY, ITHACA, NEW YORK.

FIGURE 3.
James Tanner (1914–1991) adjusts a reflector used for sound recordings of ivory-billed woodpeckers in the Singer Tract in 1935. Tanner conducted the only fully comprehensive field study of the ivory-billed woodpecker ever attempted. His intensive efforts in the Singer Tract spanned parts of four breeding seasons and were coupled with fall–winter searches for the species elsewhere in the southeastern states.

—PHOTO BY ARTHUR A. ALLEN, COURTESY OF MACAULAY LIBRARY AT THE CORNELL LAB OF ORNITHOLOGY, ITHACA, NEW YORK.

under intensive study evidently disappeared at roughly the same time, and, in practical terms, no further comprehensive biological field studies appear to have been possible in the U.S. portion of the species' range after the completion of Tanner's study.

Meanwhile, relatively brief but informative observations were made of the species in Cuba by John Dennis in 1948 and by George Lamb and his wife Nancy in 1956 (plate 3). The Lambs were still able to account for six pairs and one fledgling in a pine and hardwood region of eastern Cuba (Lamb 1957), but further study of these birds was precluded by the socialist revolution in 1959, and it was only in the mid-1980s that ornithologists returned to search intensively for the species in the region involved. By then, the total ivory-bill population was evidently down to just a very few individuals, perhaps only three. The last reasonably persuasive sighting of a single individual in this population was obtained in 1988 (see Jackson 2004).

Thus, the history of the ivory-bill in the twentieth century was quite clearly a history of inexorable decline. Early written accounts indicate that a progressive decline was also underway during the last decades of the nineteenth century. What is less certain is whether the species was also declining in early decades of the nineteenth century or in even earlier times and whether the ivory-bill had ever been a truly common species. In his monograph James Tanner (1942: 31) presented the following arguments that the ivory-bill had never been more than uncommon or rare:

> None of the early accounts of the Ivory-billed Woodpecker contained accurate or definite statements as to the abundance of the bird. Judging from the interest that naturalists and collectors had in the Ivory-bill, and the accounts they wrote, it was never common. Most writers mentioned the Ivory-bill as being a rare bird, or an uncommon one, and some heightened this picture by describing the difficulties they had in securing specimens.
>
> The one exception to this is a statement by Audubon (1842) that the Ivory-bill was "very abundant" along the Buffalo Bayou (near Houston?) Texas; he procured several specimens there. But the words "very abundant" have little meaning alone; the Ivory-bill may have been abundant there compared with the number of other birds or compared with the number of Ivory-bills in other localities. Audubon usually described the big woodpecker as being quite rare.

Tanner's belief that that the ivory-bill had always been uncommon or rare was in accord with, and in fact a major supporting justification for, his view that the species was a foraging specialist dependent on relatively uncommon sorts of food—an ecology that made individuals and pairs dependent on huge areas of pristine forest for their survival. Such an ecology in turn provided an underlying rationale for his belief that habitat destruction—logging—was likely the major factor causing progressive loss of the species.

Tanner's conclusion that the ivory-bill was a foraging specialist was based largely on his data indicating that the species usually procured food by stripping bark off recently dead trees. Recently dead trees, he contended, were a relatively scarce resource and contained few insects in comparison to the insect resources present in older dead timber. Thus, the pileated woodpecker (*Dryocopus pileatus*), which was only somewhat smaller and which was most commonly observed foraging by digging pits into older dead timber, evidently enjoyed much more abundant food supplies than were available to the ivory-bill (plate 4). By implication, the large body size of the ivory-bill, together with its large bill size, made bark-stripping behavior feasible, but at the same time a focus on bark stripping demanded that the species roam huge areas to find enough food.

In apparent harmony with the foraging differences he observed between ivory-bills and pileateds, Tanner also presented a conclusion based on the records of early specimen collectors that the maximum density of ivory-bills was only about one pair per 6 square miles of forest and that at best ivory-bills were only about 1/36 as abundant as the pileated woodpecker in high-quality woodpecker habitat. Apparently supporting these calculations, Tanner documented a home range of about 6 square miles for the one pair of ivory-bills he studied closely in the Singer Tract of Louisiana in the late 1930s, while he found as many as six pairs of pileated woodpeckers per square mile in the same region.

With such great apparent differences in the two species in maximum abundance and habitat requirements, the ivory-bill seemed likely to be much more vulnerable than the pileated to logging activities. Indeed the pileated woodpecker survives in good numbers today in second-growth forests. In contrast, Tanner documented that the disappearance of the ivory-bill from various regions in the southeastern states appeared to be quite closely correlated with the onset of logging in these regions. By the mid-twentieth century essentially all virgin forests within the range of the species in North America had been at least partially cut. Whether any U.S. ivory-bills survived beyond this date is still vigorously debated, but rigorous proof of any survivors has continued to be elusive.

Tanner's views on the causes of the species' decline have permeated virtually all modern writings on the ivory-bill and have led to an overwhelming emphasis on habitat matters in discussions of ivory-bill conservation. And while Tanner also recognized a role for human depredations in the decline of the species, especially with respect to the many birds taken by specimen collectors in several Florida river swamps, he considered depredations to be only a lesser stress. The ivory-bill has come to be regarded as one of the species most tightly dependent on pristine woodlands for its survival and most severely affected by the historical logging of bottomland forests of the southeastern states.

These views have enjoyed widespread support from the ornithological and conservation communities for more than a half century and have always appeared to be a logical, perhaps even inescapable, extension of the data available for the species. These were views that I had grown up with and accepted since I first read Tanner's monograph many years ago. They also were views that, coupled with the striking appearance of the species, provided tremendous emotional and aesthetic appeal—portraying the ivory-bill as an intrinsically rare and flamboyant wild creature that seemed to represent the very essence of towering virgin swamp forests in all their grandeur and mystery. The image of the ivory-bill given to us by Tanner is possibly the most powerful image of species endangerment and disappearing wilderness that we have. Indeed, the recent uproar that followed the potential rediscovery of the ivory-bill in Arkansas seems difficult to comprehend except as a reflection of the almost magical aura surrounding the species.

With this image of the ivory-bill in mind, however, it was more than a bit unexpected and puzzling to receive claims that this species was once a very common bird from several senior citizens familiar with it in central Florida early in the twentieth century (see Snyder 2004). I heard this viewpoint offered spontaneously during interviews conducted in 1979–81 to learn what the oldest residents of this region might know of another vanished species of southern swamps, the Carolina parakeet (*Conuropsis carolinensis*), and the information gained in these interviews held many surprises regarding the biology of that species as well.

The most informative of the people interviewed was Minor McGlaughlin, who was born in 1905 and whose personal knowledge of both parakeets and ivory-bills was extensive (plate 5). Minor grew up in the vicinity of the vast Fort Drum Swamp and participated in the lumbering of that swamp in the 1920s (plate 6). He remembered often seeing many ivory-bills during a day's activities in this swamp, and he reported that the species was once even more abundant in this location than the pileated woodpecker, an assessment of early abundance that was echoed by two other long-term residents of the region, both for the Fort Drum Swamp and for Chandler Slough farther to the southwest.

These claims, so different from those of Tanner, lay fallow in my memory for more than twenty years, but led eventually to an effort to study the written historical record closely to see if Tanner's evaluation of early rarity of the ivory-bill was truly well supported by early naturalists. The results of this investigation were presented in some detail in Snyder (2007) and are reviewed in the rest of this chapter, along with a discussion of other arguments bearing on Tanner's view of causes of the ivory-bill's decline. These materials are followed by a presentation of an alternative explanation for the species' disappearance that sadly lacks the romance of Tanner's explanation but nevertheless appears to be more consistent with the data available from historical sources.

Early Abundance of the Ivory-Billed Woodpecker

Many early naturalists commented on the status of ivory-bills in early times, and many of the early records were assembled by Edwin Hasbrouck in a review article published in the *Auk* in 1891—a review of central importance that for unknown reasons has received little attention from most modern writers on the ivory-bill. Hasbrouck, an amateur ornithologist who was professionally a surgeon for the Veterans Administration for most of his career, was one of the first to recognize that the ivory-bill was seriously declining in the late nineteenth century (fig. 4). Because of his concerns for the species, he took the trouble to correspond with other ornithologists throughout the North American range of the species to determine former status and current trends in various populations. The summary picture he presented as a result of these efforts is not one of a species that had always been rare, although the species was becoming rare in many regions at the time of his investigations.

In fact, as is clear both in Hasbrouck's report and in other historical accounts, the earliest observers of the ivory-bill quite frequently remarked on the species being common to abundant in its preferred habitat of mature swampland forests. None of the general ornithological works of the nineteenth century, including those of Alexander Wilson (1811), Thomas Nuttall (1832), John James Audubon (1842), Charles Maynard (1881), Elliot Coues (1887), and Charles Bendire (1895), claims that the species was generally scarce or rare within its normal range in early times. And even up to the time just preceding Tanner's study, Frank Chapman (1930) wrote of the ivory-bill as once having been a "locally

FIGURE 4.
Edwin Hasbrouck (1867–1956), seen here as a medical captain during World War I, spent most of his professional career as a surgeon for the Veterans Administration in Washington, DC, but he was also a dedicated amateur ornithologist and one of the first naturalists to recognize and document the degree of endangerment of ivory-billed woodpeckers and Carolina parakeets. His thorough reviews of the status of these two species in 1891 are of central importance in understanding the histories of disappearance and potential causes of decline for both species.

—PHOTO COURTESY
OF ELEANOR RAWLINGS.

common bird." Very few reports of ivory-bill rarity appeared before about 1870, and almost all of these were limited to the very edges of the species' range. After that date, however, claims of difficulty in finding the species became increasingly frequent, and by the early twentieth century, accounts claiming rarity of the ivory-bill had become predominant even for central regions of the species' range.

Overall, more than two dozen apparently independent sources (both published and unpublished) claim commonness to abundance of the species at various times and in various specific localities, representing nearly all portions of the species' North American range from southern Florida to the Carolinas in the east, across the Gulf states to Texas, and up the Mississippi River to its junction with the Ohio River. A sampling of these reports to demonstrate their timing and wide geographic distribution is given in table 1. For unknown reasons, virtually all of these reports are missing from Tanner's discussion of early numbers of ivory-bills.

TABLE 1.

Published accounts claiming commonness to abundance of ivory-bills

LOCATION	DESCRIPTION	REFERENCE
FLORIDA		
Wacissa Swamp	"quite common" in 1890	Gregg (*in* Hasbrouck 1891: 179)
	"formerly very common"	Wayne (1895: 366)
near Enterprise	"abundant" in 1850s	Bryant (1859: 11)
Gulf Hammock	"quite common" in 1880s	Laurent (1906: 67)
	"quite numerous" in 1881	Maynard (1881: 238)
Chockoloskee (?)	"plentiful" in 1877	Ellis (1917: 2)
Leon County	"formerly fairly common"	Williams (1904: 455)
Lake Jessup, other large swamps on the West Coast	"formerly common"	Boardman (1885: 388)
near St. Marks	"large numbers" until 1905	Phillips (1926: 513)
near Tarpon Spgs.	"formerly very common," now "relatively rare"	Scott (1888: 186)
GEORGIA-SOUTH CAROLINA		
Savannah River	encountered "very frequently"	Wilson (1811: 25)
near Charleston	"quite abundant" in 1851	Lawrence (*in* Hasbrouck 1891: 178)
Hunting Islands	"common" before 1870	Hoxie (*in* Hasbrouck 1891: 178)
ALABAMA		
Dallas	"not at all rare"	Gosse (1859: 91)
MISSISSIPPI	formerly "very common"	Young (*in* Hasbrouck 1891: 182)
near Houston	still "frequently met"	Young (*in* Hasbrouck 1891: 182)
LOUISIANA		
Avery Island	"still quite common"	McIlhenny (*in* Bendire 1895: 43)
TEXAS (eastern)	still "fairly common" in 1904	Bailey (*in* Oberholser 1974: 528)
Buffalo Bayou	"very abundant" in 1837	Audubon (1842: 218)
ARKANSAS		
Newport	"abundant" in 1885	Cooke (1888: 128)
KENTUCKY (western)	formerly "common"	Pindar (1889: 313)

Of special interest are the accounts of Alexander Wilson (fig. 5) and John James Audubon (fig. 6), the founding fathers of U.S. ornithology. Wilson's travels within the range of the ivory-bill were limited largely to coastal regions of the Carolinas and Georgia, and in his published account of the species he made reference to its status only along the Savannah River, separating Georgia from South Carolina (1811: 25). There he noted during a trip on horseback from Savannah to Atlanta that the ivory-bill was encountered "very frequently," a description seemingly indicating that the species was abundant in the region.

Audubon's travels in ivory-bill range were more extensive and included a float trip down the lower Mississippi River in 1820–21. In his *Birds of America* (Audubon 1842: 214, 219), he reported the species to be "common" in Texas, Louisiana, and along the Mississippi River to the Ohio River. More specifically, he wrote, "Descending the Ohio, we meet with this splendid bird for the first time near the confluence of that beautiful river and the Mississippi, after which, following the wanderings of the latter, either downwards toward the seas, or upwards in the direction of the Missouri, we frequently observe it." In northeastern Louisiana, not far from the Singer Tract, he made special note of the "constant Cry of Ivory-billed Woodpeckers about us—scarcely any other except a few Peleated [pileated woodpeckers] and Golden Wings [yellow-shafted flickers]" (Audubon 1929: 82–83).

Aside from reporting that the ivory-bill was "rare" along the lower Ohio River (which was at the very fringe of the original range of the species), Audubon clearly emphasized the general commonness of this species across much of its known range, and how Tanner could have gotten the impression that Audubon usually described the ivory-bill as "quite rare" remains a mystery. Similarly, how Audubon's remark that the species was "very abundant" in Buffalo Bayou, Texas, might be construed to imply anything other than especially conspicuous plentitude is difficult to grasp.

Other reports of conspicuous early plentitude include Bryant's (1859: 11) account of the bird as being "abundant" near Enterprise, Florida, in the 1850s; an account of G. N. Lawrence (*in* Hasbrouck 1891: 178) that the ivory-bill was "quite abundant" near Charleston, South Carolina, in 1851; an account of G. V. Young (*in* Hasbrouck 1891: 182) that the species was formerly "very common" in Mississippi; and an account of Cooke (1888: 128) that the bird was still "abundant" at Newport, Arkansas, in 1885.

FIGURE 5.
Alexander Wilson (1766–1813) of Philadelphia is generally regarded as the principal father of American ornithology and was the first naturalist to provide an extended descriptive account of the ivory-bill. One wounded ivory-bill Wilson held as a captive injured him severely with its bill and nearly escaped from his hotel room by drilling a hole through the wall. This bird lasted only three days in captivity, but its image, as painted by Wilson, lives on in his *American Ornithology* of 1811.

—ORIGINAL PORTRAIT OF WILSON HELD BY THE AMERICAN PHILOSOPHICAL SOCIETY.

Granted, the summary remarks about commonness or abundance of the ivory-bill found in early accounts were generalities lacking quantitative precision, but they were definite and meaningful remarks and should not be simply ignored or assumed to be inaccurate. The frequency and wide distribution of these remarks strongly suggest that the species was quite easy to find in early times, at least in appropriate habitat. Audubon's remarks, quoted earlier, suggest that the ivory-bill may even have been more abundant than the pileated woodpecker in one Louisiana locality, and inference similar to the reports I heard from senior citizens in central Florida and a claim that was also heard by Tanner from some early residents of the Singer Tract region. Tanner rejected such claims, but the reason he offered for doing so (people potentially underestimating the range sizes of birds) rests on a number of questionable assumptions, as discussed in Snyder (2007: 24–25).

Regardless of how one may wish to view the claims that ivory-bills were sometimes more abundant than pileateds, it seems doubtful that these claims were based on regions in which pileateds were in fact thirty-six times as abundant as ivory-bills. And unless one might wish to dismiss the honesty or competence of an impressive array of naturalists commenting on status of the ivory-bill in early times, the many accounts of the commonness and abundance of the species simply do not suggest that the ivory-bill was originally a rare species or that it was a narrow food specialist, with individuals needing huge areas of forest to satisfy their nutritional needs. Some observers (e.g., Jackson 2004) have suggested that early reports of the abundance of the species might somehow represent major overestimates, but no persuasive evidence for this appears to exist (see discussion in Snyder 2007: 26–27).

But what about Tanner's documentation of a home range of roughly 6 square miles of virgin forest for one pair of ivory-bills in the Singer Tract? Doesn't this range size in itself give evidence for huge spatial needs and intrinsic rarity of the species?

Well perhaps yes, and perhaps no. The answer depends on whether the ivory-bills in this instance were fully utilizing the food resources in their home range and whether the pair observed by Tanner might have tolerated considerable overlap in the use of its home range by other pairs. Tanner found no evidence that ivory-bill pairs defended exclusive territories, and extensive range overlap among pairs is something that is found in many bird species, for example, many raptors, parrots, and seabirds. In many of these species, individuals and pairs occupy ranges offering a considerable excess of their actual needs for food and other resources and, in many, it is simply neither feasible nor worthwhile for pairs to defend their use areas and attempt to prevent extensive simultaneous use of the same areas by other members of their own species or other potentially competing species.

For two years (1936 and 1937), Tanner (1942: 39) documented a second pair of ivory-bills simultaneously occupying the range of his closely documented pair in the Singer Tract, so it appears that amicable range overlap was indeed occurring in the species, something also suggested by observations of Scott (1888, 1898, 1903), who found eleven ivory-bills feeding simultaneously in close proximity to an active ivory-bill nest in west-central Florida in 1887. If range overlap was normal and extensive for the species, the home range sizes of individual ivory-bill pairs would tell us virtually nothing about potential densities of the species.

FIGURE 6.
John James Audubon
(1785–1851) was the United
States' most renowned early
bird artist and was captivated
by the ivory-billed wood-
pecker, which he referred
to as "Vandyke" because
of its strikingly handsome
appearance. Audubon may
well have seen more living
ivory-billed woodpeckers
than any other early ornithologist and considered the bird
"common" in swamp forests
up and down the lower
Mississippi River valley.
—ORIGINAL PAINTING BY
F. CRUIKSHANKS AND HELD BY THE
NEW YORK HISTORICAL SOCIETY.

Further, Tanner's estimate of one pair per 6 square miles as a maximum density for the ivory-bill, which led to his calculation that pileateds
were thirty-six times as abundant as ivory-bills in optimal habitat, rested
on other questionable assumptions. The primary basis for this estimate
was collecting data of Arthur T. Wayne for the Wacissa Swamp region
of northwestern Florida during 1894 (fig. 7). Wayne, a native of South
Carolina, procured nineteen ivory-bills from this swamp, and Tanner
hypothesized that he might have left on the order of half a dozen ivory-
bills uncollected there, yielding a total density estimate of about one pair
per 6.25 square miles of swamp, assuming the swamp included about
75 square miles of suitable habitat. This was the highest density Tanner
calculated for any known ivory-bill habitat, past or present.

Unfortunately, Tanner did not present supporting data for his estimate
of just six ivory-bills left after Wayne's collecting efforts. And although
the low magnitude of this estimate might seem consistent with Wayne's
(1895) published claim that the population was in severe decline from

FIGURE 7.

Arthur T. Wayne (1863–1930) was the preeminent ornithologist of the southeastern states in his day and is perhaps best remembered for his discovery, in South Carolina, of the first nests known to science of Bachman's warbler (*Vermivora bachmanii*) and Swainson's warbler (*Limnothlypis swainsonii*). A dedicated specimen collector, Wayne procured nineteen ivory-bills from the Wacissa region of Florida in 1894, and his specimens and writings constitute the most informative quantitative data on nineteenth-century abundance of this species.

—PHOTO COURTESY OF THE CHARLESTON MUSEUM.

shooting, other unpublished information provided by Wayne (but evidently not seen by Tanner) suggested that the population was nevertheless still quite large (see discussion in Snyder 2007: 12–13). Specifically, in considering the general Wacissa region in letters of August 23 and October 12, 1905, to Frank Chapman of the American Museum of Natural History (see appendix 1), Wayne indicated that the ivory-bill was still "abundant" after he finished collecting activities (in 1894) and that he knew he had "*left* more than *100* birds in a radius of *20* square miles." These remarks seem to imply many more ivory-bills than Tanner proposed for the same location and time period.

However, Wayne's use of the word *radius* in the above quotation is unusual and deserves comment, as radius generally refers to a linear, not areal, measurement. Wayne may well have been describing a region of 20 square miles surrounding some undefined location, but alternatively it seems possible that he may have envisioned a much larger region with a radius of 20 linear miles. The latter interpretation, however, poses several difficulties. A region with a radius of 20 linear miles, assuming it might be roughly circular, would imply an area on the order of 1,260 square miles. Such a large area apparently greatly exceeded the area Wayne might actually have assessed in his 1894 activities, judging in part from the time it would likely take someone heavily engaged in collecting activities to truly cover such an area, from the description of the region given in Wayne's 1895 paper, and from Tanner's (1942) calculation of only 75 square miles in the Wacissa region. In addition, one hundred ivory-bills in 1,260 square miles would yield a density of only one pair per 25 square miles, a density considerably below what anyone would likely consider "abundant." The same number of ivory-bills in 20 square miles, on the other hand, would be equivalent to 2.5 pairs per square mile—a density that might plausibly qualify as indicating true abundance because of its similarity to documented densities of pileated woodpeckers in the very best habitat (e.g., three to six pairs per square mile in the Singer Tract, according to Tanner 1942).

Thus, taken as a whole, Wayne's remarks make consistent sense only if he was truly referring to a region of just 20 square miles for his hundred-bird estimate. Moreover, assuming the validity of this interpretation, the minimum density of ivory-bills left in the region would have been fifteen times as great as Tanner's proposed "maximum" density for the species. Further, since Wayne collected nineteen ivory-bills from the Wacissa region, the minimum ivory-bill density before he began collecting might well have been close to three pairs per square mile, or about eighteen times Tanner's proposed maximum density. Even if we were to assume that Wayne's area estimate may have been quite rough and that the boundaries of the region he was referring to might actually have resembled the boundaries of Tanner's 75-square-mile Wacissa region, one hundred or more ivory-bills left in the region after Wayne finished collecting would suggest a minimum density for 1894 on the order of five times as great as Tanner's maximum density.

Giving apparent support to substantial numbers of ivory-bills still existing along the Wacissa after Wayne's collecting activities ended is the report of thirty-seven ivory-bills collected circa 1905 by J. R. Jack from the Oreilla Swamp (see Phillips 1926: 513; Jackson 2004: 72). The location of the Oreilla Swamp is obscure (I've been unable to find any other reference to a swamp of this name), although it was apparently close to St. Marks (as is the Wacissa). In his letter of October 12, 1905, to Frank Chapman, Wayne stated he did not know exactly where Jack had collected his birds, but his remarks suggest that either he or Chapman believed Jack may have collected them from the Wacissa region, and, by implication, that forty birds collected there would not likely have wiped out the population (see appendix 1).

It is also important to note that the Wacissa population could already have been substantially depleted by shooting activities of others by the time Wayne first arrived in the region. Indeed Hasbrouck (1891) documented the shooting of ivory-bills along the Wacissa in 1890, and Wayne (1895) himself reported the shooting of Wacissa ivory-bills by others for food and bill trophies at the time of his collecting activities. Thus, the original density of ivory-bills along the Wacissa before depredations began might well have been substantially larger than the population density of 1894, and the latter may have been far greater than Tanner's maximum-density estimate. These considerations raise major doubts as to the validity of Tanner's maximum-density estimate and his estimate of only a single ivory-bill pair to be expected in an area occupied by thirty-six pairs of pileateds. Both values could easily have been more than an order of magnitude too low.

Also raising doubts as to these calculations is a density estimate provided by data of M. G. Vaiden (*in* Jackson 2004: 60–62) for a population of ivory-bills still in existence in Mississippi shortly before World War II. Vaiden reported six pairs occupying 19.2 square miles of forest (a density of one pair per 3.2 square miles—nearly twice Tanner's maximum-density estimate). In similar fashion, Mason Spencer (*in* Tanner's field notes, May 17, 1937) reported the existence of ten to fifteen ivory-bills occupying the Greenlea Bend region of the Singer Tract until about 1932 (a region of approximately 6 square miles as mapped in Tanner's fig. 22), suggesting a population density that may even have exceeded one pair per square mile (six times Tanner's maximum density) if the birds involved were fully resident in the area. Tanner did not discuss either of these populations' estimates in his publications, and no independent checks are available on their validity, but both may well have represented already depleted, not pristine, populations. Taken at face value, these estimates provide additional support to the conclusion that Tanner may have greatly underestimated the early abundance of the species and greatly overestimated the space needs of populations.

Providing still more support for this conclusion is the apparent improbability that any of the many early naturalists claiming early commonness to abundance of the species might have considered Tanner's proposed maximum density—one pair per 6 square miles—to have represented commonness or abundance of the species. Tanner himself clearly did not consider the bird common at such a density. Indeed at such a density observers would generally have to travel many miles through swamp forests to encounter even a single pair, given the facts that ivory-bills were reputedly difficult to hear from more than a quarter-mile distance and that Tanner reported the birds to be silent for about half of the daylight hours when not nesting (for a quantitative analysis of potential encounter rates see Snyder 2007: 22).

Finally, that the ivory-bill may once have enjoyed densities considerably in excess of one pair per 6 square miles is made especially plausible by recent density data for another species of *Campephilus* woodpecker—the Magellanic woodpecker (*Campephilus magellanicus*)—a species of Argentina and Chile that has often been proposed as an important comparison species for the ivory-bill because of its near equivalence in size, close taxonomic relationship, and similar dependency on temperate forests (see Short 1970, 1982; Short and Horne 1990). Among all *Campephilus* species, the Magellanic is evidently the closest in size to the ivory-bill. In linear measurements it is just slightly smaller, although how these two species might compare in body weight is unclear, because only two specific weight records exist for the ivory-bill, and these are of unknown accuracy and differ substantially from each other (see Tanner 1942; Short 1982; Jackson 2002). Both of these records suggest that the ivory-bill may have been the heavier species, but how consistently and by how much are highly speculative.

In any event, Ojeda (2004) documented twelve pairs or family groups of Magellanics with extensively overlapping home ranges in a 12 square kilometer old-growth study area in Argentina. These data yield an average density of one pair or family group per square kilometer (or 2.6 pairs or family groups per square mile)—a density very similar to that evidently indicated by Wayne for Wacissa ivory-bills but roughly fifteen times as great as Tanner's proposed maximum density for the ivory-bill. Further, Ojeda emphasized that her density estimate was a minimum estimate, as she could have missed some pairs. An even higher apparent density of Magellanics was reported in the study of Short (1970)—thirteen pairs in a strip of forest approximately 0.2 square kilometers in area—a density so great (sixty-five pairs per square kilometer), one wonders if it could have resulted from highly abnormal circumstances or some error in recording of data.

Yes, it is important to note that the Magellanic does not share its range with other large woodpecker species and that an absence of close competitors could allow relatively dense populations in comparison to the ivory-bill, but it simply is not known if ivory-bill densities were ever significantly affected by sympatric populations of other large woodpeckers. Early reports of ivory-bills being more abundant than pileateds and the apparent general absence of aggression between ivory-bills and pileateds raise substantial uncertainties about such matters (see Tanner 1942: 54; discussion *in* Kilham 1972: 40–42).

The abundance of other smaller species of *Campephilus* (e.g., *C. rubricollis* and *C. melanoleucos*) has also been relatively high in some comprehensive studies of undisturbed tropical rainforests (see Terborgh et al. 1990; Thiollay 1994; and Robinson, Brawn, and Robinson 2000). These studies, conducted in Peru, French Guiana, and Panama, respectively, documented densities of *Campephilus* woodpeckers ranging from about one pair per square kilometer to as many as four pairs per square kilometer (roughly three to ten pairs per square mile). Such densities are consistent with my casual personal experiences in various Neotropical countries. For example, in a recent trip to the Iwokrama Reserve in central Guyana, I encountered the red-necked woodpecker (*C. rubricollis*) frequently along trails, with adjacent pairs often spaced on the order of a kilometer or less apart (plate 7). In view of the limited distances from which these birds could be detected in dense forested habitat, such observations suggested densities substantially greater than one pair per square kilometer.

It is also intriguing to note that in all of the above published studies in the Neotropics, *Campephilus* woodpeckers occurred in higher densities than sympatric *Dryocopus* woodpeckers (see also Slud 1964; Skutch 1969; Kilham 1972). There does not appear to be any general case to be made that *Campephilus* woodpeckers are intrinsically rare or less abundant than *Dryocopus* woodpeckers (the genus including the pileated woodpecker) where both genera occur together. The frequent numerical superiority of *Campephilus* woodpeckers raises the question of whether members of this genus might generally be less specialized in foraging than *Dryocopus* woodpeckers, something suggested as well by the apparent emphasis on ants as food by *Dryocopus* species (see Kilham 1972: 40–42).

Tanner had no personal experience with the ivory-bill as a truly common bird and seemed to have difficulty imagining the species in such a context. He was able to envision the ivory-bill as once having been somewhat more common than the density of one pair per 17 square miles of forest that he documented for the Singer Tract in 1934, but he apparently found it improbable to believe that the species could ever have rivaled the pileated woodpecker in abundance. In effect, he seemed to view the sparse Singer Tract ivory-bill population of the mid-1930s as close to the maximum possible under local forest conditions, rather than as a massively depleted remnant well below carrying capacity of forest resources. And because forest habitats were still nearly virgin in the Singer Tract and the one pair he studied closely ranged quite widely, he apparently found it compelling to assume that individuals needed huge amounts of mature forest to meet their needs. Yet as already discussed, wide-ranging behavior is often very deceptive in its overall density implications, and early ivory-bill populations may have been much denser than estimated by Tanner. The Singer Tract population may well have been far below carrying capacity of food resources due to a long decline produced by factors other than food scarcity. We will have a close look at one of these other factors—human depredations—later in the chapter.

The Ivory-Bill as a Potential Food Specialist

Tanner's belief that the ivory-billed woodpecker was an extreme foraging specialist was based primarily on his direct determination that the species fed by apparently specialized bark stripping in nearly three quarters of his observations. To be sure, Tanner also observed that the ivory-bill, much like the pileated woodpecker, sometimes foraged by drilling pits in bark-free dead timber (fig. 8; see also Pearson 1932). But the high frequency with which the species employed bark stripping led him to conclude that it had a major dependency on recently dead timber, and by implication might not be able to thrive in forests lacking substantial amounts of such timber. An ample supply of such timber seemed

FIGURE 8.

As described in James
Tanner's observations,
ivory-bills usually fed on
recently dead timber and
used bark stripping to
uncover insect prey, but
they also fed at times by
digging conical pits in
long-dead timber. This
nearly bark-free hack-
berry (*Celtis laevigata*)
trunk in the Singer Tract
was frequently worked
on by ivory-bills.

—PHOTO BY JAMES TANNER,
COURTESY OF NANCY TANNER
(TANNER 1942: PLATE 11).

to demand truly well-developed virgin forests in general—the sort of
forests that had abundant mature trees reaching the end of their life
expectancy and experiencing frequent death of branches and trunks—
the sort of forests found in regions not subjected to lumbering activities. Once forests were substantially lumbered, their timber became
converted mostly to young and healthy second growth without frequent
dead limbs and trunks and with relatively low food resources in general
for woodpeckers.

However, a high frequency of observations of ivory-bills feeding on
recently dead timber by bark stripping does not in itself demonstrate that
the species was unable to use older bark-free dead timber effectively and
does not necessarily indicate a strong dependence on recently dead timber. It may only have been a reflection of the species being well adapted
to exploit recently dead timber when it was available and the fact that

nearly all of Tanner's foraging data came from a single pair faced with an abundance of recently dead timber in its foraging range. Tanner's foraging data on ivory-bills were almost entirely limited to a pair that inhabited the John's Bayou region of the Singer Tract and, by his own direct tabulations, recently dead timber was considerably more frequent than older dead timber in this region. Timber he rated as dead four years or less (timber likely to still have bark, judging from Tanner's remarks) made up nearly 80 percent of the standing dead timber found. Over half of the dead timber was rated as dead two years or less. That the John's Bayou pair fed primarily by bark stripping may reflect little more than that dead timber still retaining bark represented a large fraction of the dead timber available for foraging. Thus from the data presented by Tanner, it is not clear that the birds fed on recently dead timber any more frequently than might be predicted by chance availability or that they had a true preference for recently dead timber.

Further, it is highly questionable that the data on frequency of foraging methods used by the John's Bayou pair should be generalized to the species as a whole. Conceivably, very different statistics on foraging methods might have been obtained if other pairs facing different timber availability situations had been studied, and there is nothing in Tanner's data to demonstrate that pairs occupying regions with much lower abundances of recently dead timber might not also have been able to prosper, mainly using foraging methods more similar to those commonly used by pileated woodpeckers. The existence of one specialized foraging technique in the ivory-bill's repertoire—bark stripping—should not be interpreted to indicate that the species was necessarily a feeding specialist as a whole, although many writers appear to have accepted this conclusion.

Indeed, reports exist of the species using a variety of other feeding techniques at different times, ranging from pileated-like digging of pits in old trunks to ground foraging like flickers, to plucking fruits and seeds from branches and vines (see Audubon 1842; Allen and Kellogg 1937). Edward McIlhenny (in Bendire 1895) even reported the species stealing acorns from squirrel nests and storing acorns in holes, presumably much like acorn woodpeckers (*Melanerpes formicivorous*). It is doubtful that the ivory-bill would have employed all these various foraging methods if it could not do so profitably.

Direct data available for the diet of the ivory-bill are relatively few, and because of this and the wide diversity of foods known to be taken by the species, they do not in themselves demonstrate food specialization. The species took both plant and animal foods and, in fact, most of the ten stomach analyses conducted with the species in historical times revealed a preponderance of plant materials (fruits and seeds) in gut contents, not insects (see Audubon 1842; Jackson 2002). Tanner's own observations of foraging ivory-bills included no instances of plant feeding, so on these grounds alone it is questionable that his data on foraging methods should be considered representative of the species as a whole.

Tanner emphasized the importance of large beetle larvae in food brought to nests, although he did not provide quantitative data on the use of such food other than in his notes on March 1, 1938, which specified "grubs" as food in ten of thirty feeding trips to a nest; foods were not identified in the other twenty trips (Tanner 1942: 74–76). Other observational data, stomach analyses, and food remains in nests indicate that the species also fed on a variety of other smaller insects (see Tanner 1942; Lamb 1957; Jackson 2002). Large beetle larvae are also common in the foods taken by pileated woodpeckers (see Bull and Jackson 1995), and how much difference there might be between these two species in kinds of foods taken has never been rigorously established. One difference that may well exist is that pileated woodpeckers are well known to feed on carpenter ants (*Camponotus* sp.), while claims that ivory-bills fed on ants are few (see Catesby 1731; Thompson 1889). Nevertheless, some ant feeding in ivory-bills seems plausible from observations of the species taking termites in Cuba (Gundlach *in* Jackson 2004: 195). Certainly pileated woodpeckers, like ivory-bills, have been known to frequently take plant materials, especially during the summer and fall seasons and, indeed, virtually all North American woodpeckers are known to feed substantially on plant materials in addition to insects (plate 8).

Recognition of broad feeding tolerances in a woodpecker species can depend importantly on the amount of diet data available. For the Magellanic woodpecker, a progression from an assumption that the species was a specialist on wood-boring insects to a later recognition that it was an opportunist taking many kinds of foods can be seen in the various papers of Ojeda and others on the species' diet. As pointed out by Ojeda (2003), the species was once believed to have a diet composed exclusively of invertebrates (Grigera, Ubeda, and Cali 1994; Rozzi et al. 1996), but her more recent data also indicated multiple instances of fruit eating and the capture of a lizard. Only three years later, after completion of food studies at seven nests, Ojeda and Chazaretta (2006) had documented not only numerous cases of Magellanics taking lizards but many cases as well of them feeding on nestling birds, birds' eggs, and even a bat. By this time Schlatter and Vergara (2005) had also documented frequent sap feeding by the species, and it had become clear that the Magellanic was indeed highly opportunistic in its foraging.

By comparison, diet data for the ivory-bill have always been much too limited to allow confidence about the full range of foods taken. Few stomach analyses have ever been performed, and only a single wild pair has been given intensive observational study. Were it possible to expand the scope of diet observations for this species, it would not be surprising to find that its diet might also include many of the more unusual food types found in recent studies of the Magellanic woodpecker.

Altogether, the data available on diet and foraging methods of the ivory-bill simply do not provide compelling evidence for strong feeding specialization. Instead, along with the evidence for early abundance of this species, they suggest that the ivory-bill may have had relatively generalized food habits similar to those of other large *Campephilus* woodpeckers. As noted by Jackson (2004: 25), the ivory-bill was likely "an opportunist, taking advantage of varying food resources." Its apparent skill in exploiting recently dead timber by bark stripping, coupled with its ability to feed in a variety of other ways, may even have given it some significant foraging advantages over the pileated woodpecker, a species apparently much less capable of bark stripping. Indeed, the pileated woodpecker, like other *Dryocopus* woodpeckers, may well be more of a food specialist than any of the *Campephilus* woodpeckers.

What Caused the Demise of the Singer Tract Population?

Between 1934 and 1938 Tanner carefully documented a progressive population decline from fourteen to six ivory-bills (not counting fledglings) in the Singer Tract—a relatively rapid decline that averaged about 17 percent per year. But contrary to the impression created by many popular accounts, at most only a small part of this decline can reasonably have been caused by timbering within the tract, since there was no timbering of any ivory-bill areas until the very end of this period (1938), and timbering initially affected only a small fraction of the tract (fig. 9). Thus, prior to the initiation of timbering, the population was steadily approaching

FIGURE 9.

Before lumbering began in the late 1930s, the Singer Tract of northeastern Louisiana was one of the largest virgin bottomland forests left in the southeastern states. Ivory-bills in the tract avoided wet regions of cypress and focused their activities in drier areas dominated by sweet gums (*Liquidambar styraciflua*) and oaks (*Quercus nuttallii*), as seen here. Belatedly, part of the Singer Tract was established as a National Wildlife Refuge in 1980, but the forests are now all second growth and empty of ivory-bills.

—PHOTO BY JAMES TANNER,
COURTESY OF NANCY TANNER
(TANNER 1942: PLATE 4).

extinction in the absence of significant human modification of available habitat, a fact that was fully recognized and discussed by Tanner. On the basis of this information alone, it appears that simple habitat preservation, although it was not formally instituted, may already have been failing as a conservation strategy for the population. It further appears likely that even had the Singer Tract been saved from all logging, the species would still have been soon lost from the region if nothing else were done to improve conditions for the species.

If not timbering, what other forces may have produced the progressive population decline in the mid-1930s? Tanner (1942: 39, 52–53) recognized that timbering did not provide a satisfactory explanation, but he argued nonetheless that the decline still could be explained "only" by a general decline in food availability—not a decline resulting from timbering, but a decline resulting from a recent absence of fire and other natural kills of large areas of timber. Thus, it appears he believed that not even the virgin old-growth forests of the Singer Tract were capable of supporting ivory-bills on a sustained basis in the absence of large-scale, food-enhancing natural disasters, such as fire or storm damage—an extreme level of dependency of the species on unusual food abundance. Tanner did provide indirect supporting data for declines in food supplies in the Singer Tract in the 1920s and 1930s that appeared consistent with the pattern of disappearance of the bird, but he did not provide data or arguments as to why he believed that decreasing food was the *only* plausible explanation for the declining ivory-bill population.

If decreasing food was in fact the correct explanation, one might expect to find some clear signs of food limitations in poor reproductive statistics of the declining population. However, ivory-bill reproduction still appeared to be reasonably strong. Tanner reported a mean overall historical clutch size of 2.9 (range 1 to 5) for the species, and during his study he documented three successful ivory-bill nests in six attempts and an average of 2.11 young for nine broods observed after fledging (figs. 10, 11). It is true that the great majority of fledglings documented in the 1930s came from just two territories, but a high variance in productivity among pairs is now known to be typical of healthy populations of many bird species (see Newton 1989). Further, assuming 50 percent nest success was normal, Tanner's population summaries (1942: 39) reveal no obvious sign of a chronic failure of Singer Tract pairs to attempt breeding, at least for the years of most intensive study (1935–39).

Tanner did not identify any pervasive reproductive problems for the Singer Tract ivory-bills, and indeed he documented almost identical reproductive output in ivory-bills as in pileated woodpeckers in the tract. Ivory-bill reproduction was high enough that low productivity was not obvious as the probable cause of the population decline. Yet low productivity caused by low clutch size, brood reductions, and nest desertions is often the first sign of difficulty in food-stressed populations. The nesting failures Tanner observed were of unknown cause and were not clearly related to food considerations. Further, he reported one ivory-bill pair with four fledglings in the Singer Tract as late as 1936, suggesting that at least this pair was doing very well from a food standpoint well into the decline. Finally, the normal daily pattern observed by Tanner (1942: 57) of ivory-bills resting quietly from mid-morning to mid-afternoon when not nesting did not suggest chronic difficulties in finding enough food.

Nevertheless, although documented reproduction in the Singer Tract was not low enough to be obvious as the major cause of the population

FIGURE 10.

A male ivory-bill of early April 1935 prepares to enter his nest in a red maple (*Acer rubrum*) in the Singer Tract. This nest apparently contained eggs at the time but was not successful, although causes of failure were not clearly established. Overall nesting productivity of ivory-bills in the tract during Tanner's studies was very similar to that of pileated woodpeckers and was not clearly a problem for the species.

—PHOTO BY ARTHUR A. ALLEN, COURTESY OF MACAULAY LIBRARY AT THE CORNELL LAB OF ORNITHOLOGY, ITHACA, NEW YORK.

FIGURE 11.

Adults frequently exchanged incubation duties at the Singer Tract ivory-
bill nest of 1935. The male characteristically incubated overnight but also
relieved his mate at intervals during the day. On average there were about
eight incubation exchanges per day and the off-duty adult often foraged
and vocalized in the near vicinity when not incubating. Nesting activities
of the Singer-Tract birds were limited to the late-winter to early-summer
period and pairs reared only one brood per year.

—PHOTO BY ARTHUR A. ALLEN, COURTESY OF MACAULAY LIBRARY
AT THE CORNELL LAB OF ORNITHOLOGY, ITHACA, NEW YORK.

decline, a downward trend in food supplies could have stimulated some birds to move away from the tract during the 1930s, thus producing a local decline by dispersal. No direct evidence for this possibility exists, but it remains an explanation worthy of consideration. Indeed, John Dennis (1967: 41) later suggested the possibility of frequent nomadic behavior in the species, representing a search for ephemeral and abundant food supplies (fig. 12). He viewed the ivory-bill as a highly mobile "disaster species," heavily dependent on such food supplies.

This view of the ivory-bill as a nomad, however, rests largely on speculation, as no marking programs were ever conducted to document long-term movements of individuals (only one individual was ever banded). It is true that ivory-bill individuals were occasionally noted in apparently new areas, suggesting dispersal from other areas (see Tanner 1942: 34–35), but such instances were quite few and may have involved only normal dispersal of relatively young birds from natal areas. It is unknown whether mature birds ever abandoned well-established home ranges. As we will see later in the chapter, the long persistence of Cuban ivory-bills in a region devastated by logging, as observed by Dennis (1948), Lamb (1957), and others, suggests strong philopatry in spite of poor habitat conditions. Audubon (1842), Maynard (1881), McIlhenny (*in* Bendire 1895), and Allen and Kellogg (1937) all believed ivory-bills to be highly sedentary. Within the Singer Tract, Tanner's data on range occupancy were also generally consistent with sedentary habits. In particular, the continued occupancy of their home range by the John's Bayou birds, even after timbering degraded this range, suggests very conservative movement patterns.

Still, it is unclear whether the progressive disappearance of ivory-bills from the Singer Tract in the 1930s was due to dispersal or mortality, or some combination of these factors. Tanner suggested that because disappearances of birds often involved pairs rather than single birds, dispersal was more likely than mortality. But this argument lacks persuasiveness if mortality were due to shooting, as Jackson (2004) documented that shooting often removed both members of ivory-bill pairs (see also the report of Pough *in* Cokinos 2000: 85). Tanner documented no cases of "new" pairs appearing in parts of the Singer Tract as pairs disappeared from other parts of the tract, and such new pairs are something one might expect to find on occasion if frequent dispersal was occurring.

FIGURE 12.
John Dennis (left) and Herbert Stoddard (right) collaborate in a search for ivory-bills in the Big Thicket of Texas in 1967. Dennis (1916–2002) had studied a breeding pair of Cuban ivory-bills in 1948, was involved in ivory-bill observations along the Chipola River of Florida in 1951, and reported finding the species in the Big Thicket in late 1966. Stoddard (1889–1968) grew up in the vicinity of Fort Christmas in central Florida, where he was closely familiar with ivory-bills in his youth and observed the species' decline before the major era of lumbering began.

—PHOTO COURTESY OF THE
ARCHIVES OF THE TALL
TIMBERS RESEARCH STATION AND
LAND CONSERVANCY.

Alternatively, the decline of Singer Tract birds in the 1930s may have been produced largely by high mortality. Endangered species are often more sensitive to mortality factors than to reproductive factors, although it is commonly far more difficult to collect data on mortality factors than data on reproductive factors because mortality events are generally very difficult to observe and document. Tanner presented no hard data on the mortality factors affecting the Singer Tract ivory-bills, and he made no quantitative analyses of whether the population decline may have been due more to mortality than to reproductive effects. Further, he provided no data on whether any important mortality factors faced by the species may have been related to food availability.

However, Tanner did mention one mortality factor that could plausibly have accounted for much and perhaps all of the decline, although this factor was presumably hard to confirm or quantify because of its illegality. Specifically, he stated (1942: 39) that there "has been some evidence, but none of it conclusive [apparently because it was second hand] that

Ivory-bills have been shot by poachers in the tract, shot more from curiosity than for any other reasons." He also provided abundant data on the extent of human depredations on the species in other areas, including the total or near total annihilation of the populations in the California Swamp and Suwannee River regions of Florida by collectors. Yet despite clearly being aware of populations wiped out by shooting, he concluded his discussion by stating (1942: 56) that the "collecting and shooting of Ivory-bills has not been the major cause of the species' decrease, has not been as important as the degradation of the Ivory-bill's habitat by logging."

The only indications Tanner's writings give as to why he dismissed shooting as a potentially dominant cause of decline are brief remarks suggesting that he believed that shooting was not sufficiently "general" and "widespread" to account for the overall decline (1942: 88, 100). He provided no evidence, however, for any substantial regions of ivory-bill habitat where shooting was absent or negligible as a threat.

Only one of the ivory-bills that disappeared from the Singer Tract in the 1930s was known to have been shot legally—the bird procured by Mason Spencer that proved the persistence of ivory-bills in this location for the ornithological world in 1932. Yet it would not have taken massive amounts of illegal specimen collecting, curiosity shooting, or subsistence poaching to have produced the population decrease observed in the 1930s. If one assumes the population might have been close to stable in the absence of shooting (an assumption neither strongly optimistic nor strongly pessimistic), the observed decline could have resulted from only about two birds shot per year—the average annual net decline. Two birds per year is much less poaching than the intensity of shooting that wiped out the California Swamp population in just two years in the 1890s (see Tanner 1942: 31). Especially in view of the large size of the Singer Tract and the problems in effectively patrolling large areas of heavy forest, obtaining proof of such relatively small amounts of poaching would likely have been very difficult.

Evidently, Tanner had no field encounters with ivory-bill poachers, but it is hard to understand on methodological grounds how he could have ruled out shooting as a major factor in the documented decline. Because he reported some interview evidence of multiple cases of ivory-bill poaching in the Singer Tract during his studies, the potential for this mortality factor to have been important in producing the local decline needs examination and analysis.

Tanner's field notes of March 22, 1937, and April 8, 1938, detail information he received from three local residents who claimed to know of substantial amounts of ivory-bill shooting in the Singer Tract during the mid-1930s. One of these was an individual who said he had heard of recent curiosity shootings of ivory-bills by ten or twelve different hunters. Assuming these hunters were not mistaking pileateds for ivory-bills, this was enough shooting in just one report to have accounted for the entire population decline of that period! Another resident reported hearing of three or four shootings of the ivory-bills during the same period, although whether these shootings were additional birds is not clear. The third resident (Mason Spencer) believed shooting was the cause of a major recent ivory-bill decline in the Greenlea Bend portion of the Singer Tract (another decline of possibly a dozen birds, but again potentially overlapping to some extent with the preceding reports). Indeed, Spencer himself may have been involved in the shooting of ivory-bills in addition to the one he was famous for collecting legally in 1932. According to Nancy Tanner (pers. comm. 2008), Spencer was responsible for maneuvering J. J. Kuhn out of his position as warden of the Singer Tract in 1938 when Kuhn refused to cooperate in allowing trophy hunting of ivory-bills by some of Spencer's friends from Baton Rouge. Kuhn was evidently replaced by three wardens (Wylie Barrow, pers. comm. 2008), but even this increased level of vigilance does not in itself guarantee that none of the very last birds were taken by collectors or other gunners.

Judging from his correspondence with A. A. Allen (letters of June 6 and 28, 1937; April 25, 1938; and June 6, 1938), Tanner was alarmed by the scale of illegal wildlife depredations in the Singer Tract, gave at least some credence to the reports of ivory-bill shootings, and was anxious to achieve much expanded warden activity in the tract. Further, in his conservation recommendations for the ivory-bill (1942: 100), he gave considerable emphasis to the importance of keeping ivory-bill regions free of shooting activities.

Additional evidence of late ivory-bill shootings in the Singer Tract was obtained by Richard Pough, who reported in 1943 (*in* Cokinos 2000: 85), "I suspect more birds than we realize have been shot around here just out of curiosity. . . . The head of the Tallulah State Police told me about his never believing there was such a bird, until [someone] brought in a pair to show [a] gang of hunters." Unfortunately, when Gilbert Pearson, president of the National Audubon Society, first publicized Spencer's 1932 "rediscovery" of ivory-bills in the Singer Tract, he mentioned to newspapers that skins of the birds were worth a thousand dollars each, very possibly stimulating increased shooting of the birds (see Tanner 1942: 56; Cokinos 2000: 80).

The reports of multiple ivory-bill shootings in the Singer Tract in the 1930s and those of ivory-bill shootings from throughout the range of the species, together with historical information on ivory-bill populations evidently devastated by shooting in Florida, make it essential that we consider human predation pressure as a possible controlling factor for all ivory-bill populations.

Historical Impacts of Human Depredations on Ivory-Billed Woodpeckers
Although virtually nothing is known about nonhuman mortality threats to the ivory-bill, many historical sources have discussed the losses of ivory-bills to shooting and other forms of human depredations. The species had multiple unfortunate characteristics that together appear to have made it one of the most vulnerable of North America's woodland birds to such pressures. As discussed in Snyder (2007), important features contributing to this vulnerability were

1. distinctive, and often steady, calling behavior, at least in early times—allowing hunters within earshot to detect, locate, and stalk the species efficiently;
2. apparent palatability;
3. large size—making the species both a relatively massive target and worthwhile as a game item;
4. frequent approachability, at least in early times;
5. frequent close spatial association of pair members (and sometimes members of family groups), leading to a potential for multiple kills per hunter encounter;
6. high value of the species for collecting and ceremonial purposes because of its conspicuous and attractive appearance, the "ivory" of its bill, and its rarity (at least in recent times);
7. demographic sensitivity to depredations, stemming from a relatively modest reproductive rate (Tanner's data suggests 50 percent nest success and about two young per successful pair per year).

Many of these factors would also apply to the pileated woodpecker, although (1), (3), (4), (5), and (6) were factors especially relevant to the ivory-bill that may have rendered it substantially more vulnerable than the pileated to human depredations. Regardless, many early pileated woodpecker populations were also heavily impacted by hunting (see Bendire 1895; Stoddard 1969; Dennis 1984; Bull and Jackson 1995).

As was well documented by numerous early observers, ivory-billed woodpeckers commonly, though not invariably, traveled as pairs or sometimes as small family groups and, likely because of restricted vision in dense forests and a need to keep together, they were known to vocalize frequently as they moved along. Tanner reported that he invariably located the birds first by hearing them, then stalking them through the forest.

Single birds, however, may have had less need for frequent vocalizing than pairs, and this consideration may underlie the relatively infrequent calls given by isolated individuals, as reported in some recent accounts (see Jackson 2004). Another factor that may be involved in lesser noisiness of birds in some recent accounts is simply the selective pressure for relative silence provided by centuries of persecution by humans (see discussion in Wiedensaul 2005: 28–29). Regardless of potential recent changes, it appears the birds were often very noisy in historical times and highly vulnerable to the gun as a result. Tanner (1942: 57) reported that non-nesting birds were generally active and noisy for about half the daylight hours. Audubon (1842: 216) wrote: "[Their calls] are heard so frequently that . . . the bird spends few minutes a day without uttering them; and this circumstance leads to its destruction . . . not because this species is a destroyer of trees but more because it is a beautiful bird, and its rich scalp attached to the upper mandible forms an ornament for the war-dress of most of our Indians, or for the shot-pouch of our squatters and hunters, by all of whom the bird is shot merely for that purpose."

Tanner also described the birds as relatively approachable, at least for their size. George Sutton, in observing a pair of the last birds in the Singer Tract, remarked, "What I remember most clearly, was the remarkable fearlessness and consequently the vulnerability of the glorious creatures. Anyone could have shot both of them easily" (*in* Dennis 1967: 43). Close approachability of the species was also suggested by Charles Maynard (1881) and by Mason Spencer (*in* Tanner field notes of March 22, 1937), who blamed the shooting of ivory-bills in the Singer Tract on the "birds' lack of intelligence." George Lamb (1957) reported a number of Cuban ivory-bills that had been stoned to death by residents, and it seems unlikely that this might have been possible with wary birds under most conditions. John Bachman (*in* Audubon 1842: 229) considered the pileated woodpecker to be "much wilder" than the ivory-bill, a belief evidently shared by Audubon.

Early approachability of the ivory-bill is also suggested by widespread killing of the species by Native Americans before guns were ubiquitous. But while the first pioneer naturalists did not report notable wariness in the species, over time, shooting pressures may very plausibly have produced such behavior in many populations through learning processes and selective elimination of relatively approachable individuals. Indeed, specific reports of especially wary ivory-bills appear to be largely limited to remnant populations that were either known or likely to have been under heavy hunting pressure (see Brewster 1881; Nehrling 1882; D. 1885; Kline 1886; Scott 1888; Elliott 1932; Tanner 1942; Lamb 1957; Short and Horne 1990). As discussed by Tanner (1942: 63), "The fact that they [ivory-bills] were pursued so constantly and avidly by collectors is probably the reason for the wary reputation of the bird. In my own experience, Ivory-bills have not been particularly shy, certainly not noticeably more wary and wild than the Pileated Woodpecker."

Jackson (2004) noted that pairs constitute a surprisingly large fraction of the ivory-bills in collections, whether caused mainly by the approachability of the birds around nests, by their tendency to travel in pairs, or by other factors. Evidently it was often possible for collectors (and presumably other shooters) to kill more than single individuals, and this potential could only have increased detrimental population effects (see Kline 1887 for one description of the ease of killing both members of a pair, resulting from the reluctance of the female to abandon her mate after he had been shot).

The ritualistic/decorative use of the species by Native Americans was evidently sufficiently widespread that trophies of ivory-bill heads and beaks were frequent items of trade. Mark Catesby (1731: 16) wrote, "The bills of these Birds are much valued by the *Canadian Indians* who make Coronets of 'em for their Princes and great warriors. . . . The Northern Indians, having none of these Birds in their own country, purchase them from the *Southern People* at the price of two, and sometimes three, Buckskins a Bill." One ivory-bill beak was even recovered from a Native

American grave in northern Colorado, far outside the range of the species (Jackson 2004). Audubon (1842: 216) saw "entire belts of Indian chiefs closely ornamented with the tufts and bills of this species." He also remarked that it was not just Native Americans who used the species in this way. He reported frontiersmen at steamboat landings displaying two or three ivory-bill heads to disembarking passengers and asking a quarter dollar for the heads. Some heads were fashioned into watch charms and fobs (Williams 1904) and, reputedly, dried ivory-bill skins were sometimes sold in European cities (Hoose 2004). From reports such as these it cannot be doubted that the species suffered from substantial human depredation pressures for trophy or totemic purposes, and it is clear that such depredations occurred long before the first settling of North America by Europeans, as well as continuing much later (see discussion *in* Jackson 2004).

In addition to trophy and totemic uses of the species, it was also killed for food, although Wilson (1811) suggested that the ivory-bill was not large enough to be worth hunting for this purpose. Nevertheless, many reports (e.g., Laurent 1917; Lamb 1957; Burleigh 1958; Eastman 1958; Stoddard 1969; as well as Lammertink et al. 1996, in a paper on the closely related imperial woodpecker) suggest widespread human predation on the ivory-bill for food. For many hunters the species evidently was large enough to eat, reputedly tasted "better than ducks," was "relished," and was considered "fine eating" (see Wayne 1895: 367; Lamb 1957: 11; Eastman 1958: 223). George Lamb (pers. comm. 2008) reported that his local sources in Cuba emphasized how delicious ivory-bills tasted "fried," and on the basis of interview information with rural Mexicans, George Plimpton (1977: 10) even entitled his article on the imperial woodpecker "Un gran pedazo de carne" (a great piece of meat). Only Laurent (1917: 65) questioned the palatability of ivory-bills, mentioning one old hunter who "found them rather poor eating."

Some of the historical shooting of ivory-bills was nothing more than curiosity shooting, as was mentioned by Tanner in discussing threats to the Singer Tract birds. Pioneer gunners evidently commonly shot the species just to get a close look at it in the hand or perhaps to hone their aim or for other random nonconsumptive reasons. Curiosity shooting may have been especially frequent in latter stages of the decline when the species had become an unfamiliar form of wildlife for many hunters. From a modern perspective, it is often difficult to appreciate just how common such reflexive shooting of wildlife used to be, as shooting nowadays is regulated much more closely. In fact, until the early twentieth century there were no laws whatsoever to discourage shooting of ivory-bills in most parts of its range, whether for scientific collecting or any other purpose. Even when laws were finally enacted, they were enforced only with mixed success, and to the present day illegal shooting remains a significant threat to many endangered species, for example, whooping cranes (*Grus americana*) and California condors (see Lewis 1995; Snyder and Snyder 2005).

Shooting losses of ivory-bills to men who collected specimens for sale to private collectors and to museums were especially well documented in the late nineteenth century when it became known that the species was becoming scarce and the value of specimens was rising. Arthur Wayne paid hunters $4 to $5 a bird for ivory-bills in the 1890s (see Tanner 1942: 55), and this was a major sum of money in those days (equivalent to about $95 to $120 in today's currency). Such incentives evidently devastated the species in locations such as the California Swamp and Suwannee River, and evidently other localities as well. Hahn (1963) and Jackson (2004) documented over four hundred scientific specimens and display mounts of ivory-bills collected over the years, many of which were originally held by wealthy private parties. Tanner (1942: 56) underestimated the number of ivory-bills in collections by about 50 percent.

Still, it is reasonable to speculate that the primary gunfire pressure on the species overall was not the relatively well-documented shooting for specimens and display mounts. Instead, it may well have been the relatively poorly documented and incidental subsistence and curiosity shooting by hunters who were in the forests primarily in search of other game species or sport—surely a much larger group of shooters overall than the specimen collectors (see Audubon 1842; Maynard 1881; Clark 1885; Lamb 1957; and Eastman 1958). The human-caused mortality of ivory-bills documented in Cuba by Lamb (1957), for example, included no examples of specimen collecting, but included many examples of subsistence, sport, and curiosity killings. Similarly, Eastman (1958) reported only cases of subsistence shooting in his interview information. The specimen collectors were almost exclusively limited to the very late nineteenth century and the start of the twentieth century in their impacts (see Jackson 2004), whereas shooting for other purposes was probably continuous since the first settlers arrived with guns in the range of the species, as indicated by Audubon (1842). For the last ivory-bill populations after about 1920, in particular, the impacts of subsistence and curiosity shooting may have greatly outweighed the impacts of specimen collectors.

Tanner (1942) evidently believed that focused specimen collecting was the only shooting threat that had ever wiped out ivory-bill populations, and he appeared to greatly underestimate the impacts of subsistence hunting on the species, mentioning only Wayne's (1895) account. In this judgment he may have been importantly influenced by Frank Chapman (1930), who denied any role at all for subsistence hunting of ivory-bills and doubted that collecting and wanton shooting were enough to have produced the overall decline.

Despite the skepticism of Tanner and Chapman, the many and diverse accounts of human predation on ivory-bills, the widespread distribution of such pressures, and the clearly devastating impacts of such depredations on some populations give plausibility to the hypothesis that human predation pressure has been a major factor in the decline of all wild populations of the species. This is not a new hypothesis, and indeed shooting was considered a major stress or cause of the species' decline by Audubon (1842), Maynard (1881), Wayne (1895), Pearson (1932), and many others in early times. In more recent times it was also considered the major cause of decline by Herbert Stoddard (1889–1968), one of the most knowledgeable observers of the species in northern Florida and southern Georgia in both the late nineteenth and early twentieth centuries. Whitney Eastman (1958), who investigated historical reports of the species in the 1950s and documented multiple cases of subsistence shooting in interviews, likewise thought it was the major problem. Similarly, in a study of the closely related imperial woodpecker of Mexico, based largely on interviews of long-time rural residents of the Sierra Madre Occidental, Lammertink et al. (1996: 41) concluded that the extirpation of that species in many regions was due more to human depredations than to habitat degradation, a conclusion also reached on many other grounds in the next chapter of this book.

No substantial regions of ivory-bill range have been identified where human depredation pressures were absent, and it does not seem at all unreasonable to suggest that the overall high vulnerability of the species to such pressures may well have sealed its doom. The substantial number of reports of how shy the very last few ivory-bills were in various populations (e.g., Brewster 1881; Nehrling 1882; D. 1885; Kline 1886; Scott 1888; Elliott 1932; Short and Horne 1990), contrasting with reports of historical approachability of the species in the same and other regions, strongly suggest significant impacts of human predation pressure in the history of decline. They are not something predicted by other decline hypotheses, such as habitat degradation or food limitation.

Interactions of Various Potential Causes of Decline

It is worth considering that the most crucial negative effect of timbering on the ivory-bill may not have been a decrease in food supplies, but an increase in shooting of the species due to improved access to forests provided by lumber roads and to the substantially increased numbers of people frequenting the forests because of timbering activities. Such increased predation may go a long way toward explaining the close correlation in time of the final loss of various ivory-bill populations with the advent of timbering that was documented by Tanner (1942). In a similar vein, Bennett and Gumal (2001), Fimbel, Grajal, and Robinson (2001), Mason and Thiollay (2001), Rumiz et al. (2001), and Wilkie et al. (2001) have recently documented a major facilitation of overhunting of wildlife caused by logging activities in tropical rainforests. As discussed by these authors, the increased hunting that usually accompanies selective logging operations can often have far more detrimental effects on vulnerable species than the changes in forest structure and food supplies that are produced by the logging.

It is also important to recognize here that Tanner's correlation between the timing of the disappearance of ivory-bill populations and the advent of timbering concerned only the *final* disappearance of these populations. In at least a substantial number of regions, evidence was strong that the birds were already largely eliminated prior to the advent of major timbering operations (e.g., the Singer Tract, the California Swamp, the Gulf Hammock, the Suwannee River, the Santee River bottoms—see Tanner 1942 and notes; Stoddard 1969), and the same may have been true of most regions. Cases in which ivory-bill populations were known still to be appreciable in size immediately prior to timbering are very few (McIlhenny 1941; M. G. Vaiden *in* Jackson 2004: 60–62) and, even in these cases, facilitation of shooting (although not documented) could have been the most important detrimental effect of timbering on the birds.

Hasbrouck (1891) was stimulated to conduct his thorough early review of the status of the ivory-bill by widespread feelings that mainland ivory-bills were already becoming scarce in the 1870s and 1880s. Yet although considerable clearance of forested lands occurred during this period (see Askins 2000), Tanner (1942: ch. 4) concluded that massive lumbering operations of the bottomland swamp forests generally considered to be primary ivory-bill habitat began only in the 1890s and 1900s in many parts of the Southeast and even later in many specific regions. It is true that Short (1982) suggested that mainland ivory-bills may originally have been associated primarily with southern pine forests rather than bottomland swamp forests, but such a potential association does not appear to be supported by accounts preceding the major cutting of southern pine forests, such as those of Wilson (1811) and Audubon (1842), which characterized the ivory-bill as primarily a bird of the southern swamps and bottomlands. Maynard (1881: 238) specifically noted that the species was seldom found in "piney woods," and Tanner himself considered swamp woodlands to be the primary habitat of the species, as did virtually all other writers on North American populations of the species in early times. Ivory-bill use of pine forests was evidently much better developed in Cuba and, likewise, the imperial woodpecker was primarily an occupant of pine forests in Mexico, as will be considered in the next chapter.

Tanner reported that the biggest increase in lumbering of bottomland swamp forests did not take place until after 1900 in both Florida and Louisiana, yet as documented by many sources, the species was already greatly reduced in much of Florida by 1890 (see Maynard 1881; Hasbrouck 1891). Here, and in at least some other regions, it appears likely that the bird was largely gone before lumbering would have had a chance to cause a major drop in its food supplies. So, although straggling individuals and certain small populations lasted into the era of massive lumbering, it is questionable that lumbering was the major cause of decline, simply because of timing.

The gap between the timing of major population declines and onset of logging of bottomland swamp forests was especially well documented for the Singer Tract of Louisiana, where major indiscriminate shooting pressures on wildlife clearly preceded timbering activities. Tanner (1942: 37) reported "heavy" hunting activity in the tract in the decades before 1920, and in his March 24, 1937, field notes he quoted J. J. Kuhn, his chief assistant in field studies, as remarking that ivory-bills were among the species shot "frequently" in those early years. Kuhn reported that "One man killed six in one morning in trying out a new rifle" and that "the area was hunted intensively by large parties, sometimes killing incredible numbers of squirrels, deer, and turkey." Specimen collectors were also active in the region. Hahn (1963) tabulated a number of ivory-bills collected from Madison Parish (the location of the Singer Tract) in early decades of the twentieth century and, in mid-July 1899, George Beyer (1900) procured seven ivory-bills near Big Lake of nearby Franklin Parish after seeing the head of an ivory-bill in the possession of a local resident.

Even after the Singer Tract became a wildlife sanctuary in 1920, poaching remained a continuous problem, and by the time timbering started in the late 1930s, there were virtually no ivory-bills left, as documented in detail by Tanner (1942). Yet somehow, timbering is still generally blamed for the loss of the species in the Singer Tract, and most accounts of the disappearance of this population (e.g., Hoose 2004) dwell only on the undeniably tragic failure to stop logging of the tract as the very last birds disappeared.

Tanner succeeded in maintaining a food-limitation hypothesis for the Singer Tract ivory-bills by suggesting that the forests of the tract were suffering a major progressive decline in availability of food prior to the onset of logging. But aside from the uncertainty of whether this potential decline was a significant stress for the Singer Tract ivory-bills (something that was not apparent in reproductive statistics), such an explanation is difficult to apply to the entire range of the ivory-bill, as it seems highly questionable that massive declines in food availability might have been widespread among bottomland forests prior to the major era of timbering of these forests.

If, on the other hand, we allow the possibility that the decline in the Singer Tract in the 1930s was produced mainly by poaching, there would be no impetus to conclude that the largely virgin forests of the tract were in any way inadequate foraging grounds for ivory-bills prior to timbering, and no necessity to postulate that the species could persist in the tract only if large-scale, food-enhancing perturbations such as fire and storm damage of timber were to occur with some frequency. Tanner's suggestion that the virgin forests of the Singer Tract may not have been adequate foraging grounds for the species in the absence of such recurrent natural disasters was not based on any direct evidence of food problems in the declining population and appears instead to be an ad hoc hypothesis invoked to explain an ivory-bill decline occurring in the absence of timbering.

Records do exist of ivory-bills feeding on the insect resources in timber tracts killed by fire or other disasters (e.g., Wayne 1893; Allen and Kellogg 1937; Scott 1898) but such records are not abundant enough to demonstrate a major or obligatory association of the species with such resources. Moreover, they do not differentiate the ivory-bill from many other woodpecker species known to be attracted at times to such resources but not clearly dependent on them in a major way, given that these species are also widespread and common in forests lacking such resources. In particular, records of ivory-bills feeding on disaster-killed timber appear to be no more frequent than records of pileated woodpeckers feeding on such timber (e.g., Audubon 1842; Bendire 1895; Moseley 1928; Kilham 1976; Schardien and Jackson 1978), yet the pileated is not normally considered to be a "disaster species." Even species such as the black-backed woodpecker (*Picoides arcticus*) and the three-toed woodpeckers (*Picoides tridactylus*) that are famed for their associations with tracts of disaster-killed timber are also known to occupy forests that lack such resources (Dixon and Saab 2000; Leonard 2001).

Early descriptions of ivory-bill habitat associations in North America, such as those of John Abbott (*in* Jackson 2004: 100), Wilson (1811), Audubon (1842), Maynard (1881), Hasbrouck (1891), and McIlhenny (1941) suggest a strong association of the species with mature swamp forests. If the ivory-bill had truly been primarily dependent on disaster-killed timber tracts, one would expect to find this relationship mentioned frequently in the early historical record and to find numerous reports of ephemeral assemblages of ivory-bills in such habitats. But instead, one finds mostly reports of relatively dispersed and stable associations of ivory-bills with mature forest tracts.

It is reasonable to believe that timbering would generally have lowered food supplies and the carrying capacities of affected forests for ivory-bills, but it is not at all clear that the quite selective cutting typical of the late nineteenth and early twentieth centuries would generally have lowered carrying capacities to zero. In that era, trees were cut laboriously by hand saws, not chain saws. Snags and other defective trees containing much food for woodpeckers were often left standing. Further, as discussed by Hill (2007: 56–58), cutting in many southern swamps was limited largely to accessible cypress (*Taxodium distichum* or *ascendens*)—not a favored food tree of the ivory-bill in Tanner's studies. With food supplies only degraded, not eliminated, a reasonable possibility appears to exist that many ivory-bill populations in logged regions might still have found enough food to persist and might have endured at modest densities, had they been free of shooting pressure. The long persistence of the ivory-bill in one quite thoroughly logged region of Cuba supports this possibility, as will be discussed next.

Implications of Habitat Associations of the Ivory-Bills on Cuba

The central assumption of Tanner's view of the ivory-bill is that the species was dependent on huge areas of largely virgin forest to obtain enough food. Virtually all of the last reports of ivory-bills on the mainland came from old-growth forests, and this correlation provides perhaps the strongest argument in favor of Tanner's position. However, this correlation can be explained alternatively as a result of remote virgin forests being the regions where human depredations were least prevalent. Further, this correlation is much less clear for the ivory-bills of Cuba, and indeed most of the last sightings of the species on this island came from forests devastated by lumbering activities (plate 9). These reports all emerged after Tanner had published his monograph on the species, and had he been aware of the situation on Cuba, it is possible that his monograph might have been quite different in its conclusions.

Originally, ivory-bills appear to have been distributed nearly island-wide in Cuba, but steady clearance of arable lands for agriculture removed the forest cover from vast regions by the late nineteenth century, and by the early twentieth century reports of the species were limited to a few mountainous regions (Barbour 1943; Jackson 2004). By the time of Tanner's ivory-bill studies in the United States, some observers considered the Cuban birds extinct (Moreno Bonilla 1938).

Nevertheless, ivory-bills were rediscovered in northeastern Cuba by John Dennis in 1948. Dennis found a breeding pair and extra bird in the hills south of Moa, where they were occupying habitat that had been thoroughly lumbered some seven years earlier and was now largely open fields studded with young pines and pine snags that had not been removed during the lumbering operations. In the absence of knowledge that ivory-bills were actually present, one can reasonably assume that such habitat would have been immediately ruled out as potential ivory-bill habitat by believers in dependency of the species on virgin forests. Yet the fact that ivory-bills were even nesting in such habitat should make us wonder why the ivory-bill had not survived in many selectively timbered forests on the mainland that were apparently in much better shape.

The association of Cuban ivory-bills with devastated habitat was confirmed for the same region in a follow-up study in 1956 by George and Nancy Lamb. Four of the six pairs described in the published report of this study (1957) were in heavily cutover lands, and the forests in the remaining two territories (at the southernmost fringe of the study area) were in the process of being cut at the time of this study. Yet even in the heavily cutover areas, George Lamb considered ivory-bill food to be "fairly plentiful" due to the many fires occurring in the regenerating pine forests and the subsequent infestation of the dead trees by beetle larvae. He was much more concerned about progressive loss of nesting and roosting sites, as the standing snags remaining after lumbering operations were steadily being lost through decay. To counter this problem, he even recommended the possibility of installing nest boxes in the region. In any event, there was still some reproduction going on among the birds in the cutover lands studied by both Dennis and Lamb, and it appears the birds must still have been finding at least minimally adequate amounts of food for this to be true.

Highly degraded habitat conditions were still reported when the last few individuals of the species were seen in part of the same region in the middle to late 1980s (Short and Horne 1990; Jackson 2004). In fact, these birds were occupying one of Lamb's active territories (Ojito de Agua) that had been heavily lumbered in the 1950s. Lammertink (1992) speculated that these birds may have moved into this area from another of Lamb's ivory-bill territories (Nuevo Mundo), when the latter was heavily lumbered in the early 1980s, but, alternatively, birds may well have occupied Ojito de Agua continuously since the 1950s. Lamb reported that Nuevo Mundo was already being lumbered for a second time in the 1950s, and it is unclear how well timbered it may have been in the early 1980s or whether birds were even still present there at that time.

How are we to rationalize the surprisingly long persistence of the last known Cuban population in degraded habitat? One speculative possibility is that the birds in the region studied by Lamb may have represented a population sustained by spillover production from some relatively well-forested source area or areas outside this region. But the fact that

Lamb found one pair in exactly the same cutover forest where Dennis had found a nesting pair eight years earlier (the Bandolero area), and that this same area was also known to have hosted a nesting pair seven years before Dennis's study when lumbering activities were being conducted, suggested long-term occupancy of this area, potentially stretching back into prelumbering times. Rather than representing pairs moving into the area from other locations, the birds observed there by Dennis and Lamb seem more likely to have been a single indigenous pair (possibly with some mate replacements over the years), demonstrating lasting territorial tenacity despite massive habitat degradation years earlier.

Likewise, territorial tenacity seems a reasonable explanation for the presence of birds in Ojito de Agua both in 1956 and in the middle to late 1980s, despite lumbering of this area in the late 1950s. None of the relatively recent searches for well-forested areas near Lamb's study region have turned up additional ivory-bills, and the few areas of good forest found have been only relatively small patches with unknown histories of occupancy by the species (see Lammertink and Estrada 1995). Thus, persuasive evidence is lacking that the birds found in degraded habitat by Lamb and others may have come from good habitat elsewhere. Instead, the last birds in this region may all have begun and ended their careers in the same region.

Another suggestion worth considering is that the Cuban population may have had much broader food tolerances than found on the mainland due to the absence of any similar-sized competing woodpeckers on the island (pileated woodpeckers do not occur on Cuba). If so, the species may have been much better adapted to withstand habitat degradation on Cuba. However, direct data on the feeding habits of Cuban and mainland ivory-bill populations do not reveal any conspicuous differences either in feeding behavior or diet, although data are admittedly too skimpy to test this question rigorously.

In size and coloration, the Cuban and mainland forms of the species are very similar, and the only morphological difference of any apparent significance that has been reported is a slightly shorter average bill length in the Cuban population, perhaps a reflection of the birds generally feeding on smaller trees in Cuba. In other woodpeckers that have been studied in island situations where they have lacked a normal complement of competitor species, bill size has sometimes diverged greatly between sexes as an apparent evolutionary response that broadens the foods available for pairs (Selander 1966). Greater sexual bill-size dimorphism in Cuban ivory-bills would provide some evidence for an expanded food niche if it were true but, instead, available specimens appear to show somewhat less sexual bill-size dimorphism in the Cuban population than in mainland populations (see data in Jackson 2002). Thus, good evidence for expanded foraging capacities in the Cuban birds has not been assembled, and although it still remains possible that the ivory-bills on Cuba have faced a generally more favorable food situation in degraded habitats than have ivory-bills on the mainland, the opposite situation also remains possible.

Instead, what does appear to be distinctly different about degraded habitats on Cuba and the mainland is the amount of shooting pressure on wildlife species. A real possibility exists that the relatively long survival of the Cuban population was due in large part to relatively modest levels of human depredations on that population. Consistent with this possibility, available information appears to indicate that shooting was only an infrequent activity in the region occupied by the last Cuban ivory-bills before the revolution of 1959 (George Lamb, pers. comm. 2008) and has been greatly reduced by governmental policies since then. Guns appear to have always been relatively scarce in the region, and although Lamb (1957) reported a substantial number of recent killings of Cuban ivory-bills, many were by means other than shooting. Among the alternative methods used, the birds were sometimes killed by stoning or by stuffing the entrances of roost or nest holes with sacks on the ends of poles to trap birds within, then felling the trees—presumably relatively difficult and unreliable ways to kill ivory-bills that would not have been necessary had guns been readily available.

Nevertheless, it still seems plausible that the losses to various forms of human predation may have been long-standing and frequent enough to account for eventual extirpation of the last Cuban population. In unpublished letters of 1944 and 1948 (James Wiley, pers. comm. 2006), the ornithologist Charles Ramsden considered depredations for curiosity and food to be a significant stress on Cuban ivory-bills in the early twentieth century—he collected several specimens himself. Dennis (1948) similarly reported problems with depredations for the last known population. For the same population, Lamb (1957) documented three individuals killed for sport, eight killed for food, three killed out of curiosity, and two killed for unknown reasons. In addition, one nestling died after it was removed from a nest. Although derived from reports over a ten-year period, these losses (seventeen birds altogether), exceeded the number of birds (thirteen) in Lamb's study area at the time of his investigations (1956), and it is questionable that the population could have withstood such stress in the long run.

Assuming rough stability of the population in the absence of depredations, one can compute that the rate of depredations may have averaged about 8 percent of the population per year and that projected into the future, this rate would have been more than adequate to have produced the entire population decline documented by the middle to late 1980s. In fact under this rate, the population should have reached effective extinction (fewer than two birds left) by the end of the 1970s.

Whatever the actual rate of human depredations may have been in the 1960s and 1970s, Short and Horne (1990) reported interview evidence that killing of Cuban ivory-bills for food continued until the 1980s and that the very last birds were exceedingly wary because of hunting activities. By comparison, Dennis characterized the birds as being quite approachable in 1948, while Lamb (1957: 11) reported, "some of the remaining pairs have become very wild . . . possibly because of previous unsuccessful attacks by stoners." Thus, despite apparent increasing wariness of the birds, human depredations evidently continued until virtual elimination of the population and are quite plausible as the major cause of the population's disappearance.

However, it is also true that the quality of the last Cuban ivory-bill habitat was far from optimal and was deteriorating from the 1940s to the 1980s, so it is difficult to rule out poor habitat quality as having some importance in the decline, especially in view of Lamb's (1957) documentation of only a single apparent fledgling produced by six pairs in 1956. From the reports and photographs available, it appears that the degradation of pine forests occurring in the twentieth century in the last Cuban ivory-bill range may have been considerably more thorough and severe than the forest degradation that resulted from selective lumbering of many bottomland forests of mainland United States during the late nineteenth and early twentieth centuries. Lamb (1957) reported that all pine trees greater than six inches in diameter were being taken in Cuban lumbering operations (presumably with the exception of twisted and otherwise flawed trees; see plate 9).

Whatever the relative contributions of depredations and habitat destruction may have been toward the decline of the Cuban population from the 1950s to the 1980s, it is intriguing to note that this population declined at only about half the rate documented for the population in the Singer Tract from 1934 to 1938 (roughly 7–8 percent annually versus 17 percent annually), despite the virtual absence of habitat loss in the Singer Tract during this period and the near complete habitat degradation characterizing the Cuban population during its final decline. It seems counterintuitive that the difference in rate of decline between these two populations might trace mainly to the differences in amount or rate of habitat destruction, as this cause would presumably have led to a much faster decline in the Cuban population than in the Singer Tract. Much more plausible is the possibility that the difference in rate of decline resulted mainly from more intense shooting pressure in the Singer Tract than in Cuba.

The importance of Dennis's Cuba observations was well recognized in portions of a letter of Herbert Stoddard to John Baker, the executive director of the National Audubon Society, dated September 24, 1951 (Stoddard 1951; courtesy of A. Sprunt IV, 1979).

I received the Allen-Tanner report, and . . . I must say after a careful reading of this report that I am proceeding on several opposite assumptions than these good friends of mine. I have always had a very strong "hunch" that the ivory-bills have been as much or more "shot-out" by man from the earliest pioneer days, as reduced by environmental changes; although the latter may, of course, have a profound influence. I think my feeling in this has been somewhat strengthened by the Dennis finding of the Cuban ivory-bills nesting in an environment devastated to the limit by lumbering and uncontrolled fires. After all, this is only a subspecies of our bird. . . . I lived so long in the real Florida "flatwoods" before the lumbering days that I know from personal experience just how great shotgun pressures were from the lawless alligator hunters and other hombres that curried [combed] every mile of the wildest swamps, shotguns in hand and all year around, previous to 1900. They came very near killing out all the deer, wild turkeys, egrets and all the rest of the large and striking creatures now staging such a spectacular comeback. . . . I am still figuring that the shotgun did it.

In these few sentences, Stoddard (fig. 12) admirably touched upon many of the most important arguments for human depredations as the most crucial factor in the disappearance of the ivory-bill, and the fact that his judgments were based in part on substantial personal experience with the species and its habitat before widespread logging began is worth emphasizing. Stoddard's vivid description of pre-1900 hunting pressures (see also Stoddard 1969: 23) echoes that found in Joseph Allen's (1876) earlier account, and for a species as vulnerable to shooting as the ivory-bill, one wonders how survival might have been possible in the long run in areas inhabited by people unless deliberate and major efforts to prevent depredations might have been undertaken. Stoddard's words speak forcefully for the personal orientation of all three authors of the present volume toward the disappearance of both the ivory-billed woodpecker and the imperial woodpecker.

Comparisons with the Imperial Woodpecker of Mexico

As a final important component to any analysis of the ivory-bill's decline, it is intriguing to consider that even though Tanner did not provide a thorough discussion of his reasons for dismissing human predation pressure as the major stress for this species, he considered human predation, not habitat degradation, to be the main cause of decline of the closely related imperial woodpecker in Mexico (1964). Tanner did not personally observe imperials, but two decades after completion of his ivory-bill studies he did conduct a field assessment of this other species based on interviews and a personal look at remaining habitat in Durango. His conclusions as to causes of decline rested mainly on (1) the fact that prior to significant habitat degradation, imperials had disappeared from a number of the forested areas he investigated, and (2) the fact that interview information he obtained suggested substantial shooting pressures on the species. But although the same features appeared to have been true for the ivory-bill in at least a considerable number of regions of the United States, including the Singer Tract, Tanner made no formal comparison of the causes of decline of the two species in his imperial woodpecker paper and offered no retrospective modification of his judgment as to overall causes of the ivory-bill's decline.

Tanner did mention several historical and interview accounts that the imperial woodpecker had once been common, and he did remark

(1964: 77) that "the American Ivory-bill obtains most of its food by knocking the bark from recently dead trees" and that "the Imperial Woodpecker feeds to some extent in this manner, but differs from the Ivory-bill in feeding extensively in long-dead, decaying trees." These remarks strongly suggest that he was still a supporter of food specialization in the ivory-bill but was not making exactly the same case with the imperial woodpecker, although just as for the ivory-bill, he estimated very low densities for the imperial—one pair per 10 square miles—potentially a massive underestimate, as discussed in the next chapter. Regardless, the basic depredations argument he presented for the imperial woodpecker's decline is the same as the argument presented here for the ivory-bill's decline, and whether there was really a fundamental difference in foraging methods used by the two species is by no means certain.

Summary

In most recent accounts the extinction or near extinction of the ivory-billed woodpecker has been attributed mainly to extreme foraging specialization that did not allow the species to adapt to the degradation of virgin forests within its range, an explanation most comprehensively developed by Tanner (1942). In this chapter, however, I discuss the possibility that the species may not have been a food specialist overall and consider an alternative primary cause of endangerment—human predation pressure—a stress emphasized by many early naturalists.

The human predation alternative poses no inconsistencies with the numerous historical writings indicating early abundance of the species. It further appears fully consistent with the reputed high vulnerability of the species to depredations, with numerous and widespread early accounts of ivory-bill losses to shooting and other forms of human depredations, with the complete or near complete loss of certain populations prior to timbering activities, and with the relative wariness of the very last individuals in many (although not all) remnant populations. Enough quantitative data exist on certain populations (e.g., the California Swamp, Singer Tract, and last known Cuban populations) to allow a conclusion that human depredations alone could plausibly have caused extirpation without a need to invoke any other stress factors. And although human depredations do not preclude the simultaneous existence of feeding specializations, they may well have been sufficiently pervasive and chronic to have continuously depressed populations below a level where feeding limitations might have had any major role in producing the species' decline.

In contrast, the food-specialization hypothesis is not in harmony with the numerous reports of early ivory-bill commonness or abundance, with the complete or near complete disappearance of some populations prior to timbering, with the long persistence of the last known Cuban population in devastated habitat, and with the substantial flexibility in foraging behavior and diet reported for the species. These problems make it uncertain that feeding specialization played any major role in decline of the species.

Hypotheses of extreme food specialization and early rarity of the ivory-bill are difficult to sustain without rejection of the claims of many early naturalists that the species was once common to abundant. Yet no persuasive grounds for dismissing these claims have yet been put forth, and ignoring these claims is equivalent to dismissing them without justification. Density of the very last remnant ivory-bill population in Louisiana in the mid-1930s should not be assumed to represent anything like the density typical for the species in earlier times, nor should the last population simply be assumed to have been at carrying capacity of food resources. Food is only one of a diversity of factors that can limit bird populations, and many endangered species are known to be stressed primarily by other factors. That the decline of the ivory-bill in the Singer Tract largely preceded timbering or other major modifications of forested habitat raises serious doubts that the decline was mediated primarily by food considerations, especially when this decline is considered alongside major declines of the species preceding timbering in other regions.

Tanner's beliefs that the maximum density of the ivory-bill was about one pair per 6 square miles (15.5 square kilometers) and that pileated woodpeckers were roughly thirty-six times more abundant than ivory-bills at maximum density are not well confirmed by available historical data. Both conclusions rested on Arthur Wayne's ivory-bill collecting data from the Wacissa Swamp of Florida in 1894. But judging from Wayne's correspondence of 1905 (appendix 1), Tanner's estimate of the number of ivory-bills in this location may have been only a small fraction of the true total. Further, the Wacissa population at that time may already have been substantially depleted by earlier shooting activities. Both factors suggest that the original density of ivory-bills in the region may have been far greater than estimated by Tanner.

Other early accounts also suggest that ivory-bill densities were often much higher than one pair per 6 square miles, perhaps sometimes even more than an order of magnitude higher, although no rigorous estimates of maximum regional densities are available. Further, a variety of reports and reasonable inference generally support the possibility that in early times the species may not have differed greatly from the pileated woodpecker in its population densities, at least in southern bottomland forests. The densities of other *Campephilus* woodpeckers studied in old-growth habitats of South America in recent years have often exceeded those of sympatric *Dryocopus* woodpeckers and have often been in or above the general range documented by Tanner for pileated woodpeckers in the Singer Tract. The Magellanic woodpecker (*Campephilus magellanicus*), often considered a South American ecological counterpart of the ivory-bill, has been documented in one recent study at a density approaching three pairs per square mile. That the ivory-bill may once have achieved similar densities should not be considered unreasonable. The large home range that Tanner documented for one ivory-bill pair in the Singer Tract is not inconsistent with such densities if home ranges overlapped extensively. Available evidence suggests that ivory-bills did not defend home ranges and that pairs did overlap in their use of space, as has also been documented in the Magellanic woodpecker.

Tanner's behavioral observations and reproductive statistics for the last ivory-bill population in Louisiana do not suggest the obvious problems with food stress that might be expected under the food specialization hypothesis. And although logging may well have had negative effects on the last ivory-bill populations, logging was often quite selective in early times, leaving untouched most snags and defective trees, the sources of much of the food taken by woodpeckers. Many ivory-bill populations were evidently already strongly reduced by the time logging began, and the most important negative effects of logging may not have been reductions in food supplies, but the facilitation of shooting of the species through construction of lumber roads and through sponsorship of greatly increased numbers of people in forested habitats.

Thus, available information and reasonable inference appear to support human predation pressure, likely exacerbated by habitat degradation, as a more plausible primary explanation than the traditional explanations of food specialization and habitat degradation in accounting for the decline of the ivory-bill. And if losses to human predation were indeed the major factor, it may well be that the ivory-bill was not crucially dependent either on huge areas of virgin forests or on natural disasters for adequate food. Its apparent limitation to uncut forests as extinction approached (at least in the United States) may instead have been a secondary correlation resulting mainly or in part from the degree of protection from human depredations offered by remote forests. The better survival of the pileated woodpecker to the present may be due primarily to its lesser vulnerability to human depredations and not to any basic superiority of this species in procuring food.

PLATE 1.

The third largest woodpecker in the world, the ivory-billed woodpecker (*Campephilus principalis*) of the southeastern United States and Cuba, was once reputedly a common inhabitant of towering bottomland swamp forests but also made some use of pine forests. Adult males had brilliant red crests, while females and fledgling males had black crests.

—PAINTING BY NARCA MOORE-CRAIG, PORTAL, ARIZONA.

PLATE 2.

Toby Creek, a tributary of Wadmacaun Creek and the Santee River in South Carolina, was a location still frequented by ivory-bills in the late 1930s. The large cypress (*Taxodium distichum*) in this photograph of 2003 was also photographed some sixty-five years earlier by Alexander Sprunt, Jr., as an "Old Patriarch" (see Snyder 2004: 63). Despite logging, the swamp forests of the region still retain many giant trees and dense populations of pileated woodpeckers (*Dryocopus pileatus*), but ivory-bills have not been seen here for many years.

—PHOTO BY N. F. R. SNYDER.

PLATE 3.

With his wife Nancy, George Lamb (1928–present) conducted a single-season study of the Cuban ivory-billed woodpecker in 1956 and found evidence for six pairs and a fledgling in a heavily logged region near the eastern end of the island—the same region where John Dennis had rediscovered the species and studied a nesting pair in 1948. In much earlier times, ivory-bills had been found throughout lowland forested regions of the island.

—PHOTO COURTESY OF GEORGE LAMB.

PLATE 4.

The pileated woodpecker (*Dryocopus pileatus*) is a large black and white species found throughout much of the range of the ivory-bill. Only slightly smaller than the ivory-bill, it too shows considerable white in the wings in flight, although the white wing patches largely disappear from view in perched birds, as seen in this photograph. However, occasional aberrant pileateds have extensive white wing patches closely resembling those of perched ivory-bills, making them difficult to identify correctly unless detailed characteristics of the head and bill are also clearly visible. James Tanner focused on ecological and behavioral comparisons of pileateds with ivory-bills in his monograph of 1942.

—PHOTO COURTESY OF RON AUSTING.

PLATE 5.

Minor McGlaughlin (right) in conversation with Rod Chandler of the National Audubon Society in 1981. As a former cattle rancher, logger, plume-hunter, and moonshiner from Okeechobee County in central southern Florida, Minor (1905–1988) remembered ivory-bills as even more common than pileated woodpeckers in Fort Drum Swamp early in the twentieth century. This claim, so contrary to conventional wisdom of today, served as a primary stimulus for the ivory-bill research summarized in this book.

—PHOTO BY N. F. R. SNYDER.

PLATE 6.

Fort Drum Swamp, north of Lake Okeechobee, was renowned as a former home for both Carolina parakeets and ivory-billed woodpeckers but was logged of its largest cypress trees in the 1920s to make railroad ties. Abandoned defective ties could still be found half submerged in the swamp, virtually undeteriorated by age, when this photo was taken in 1980.

—PHOTO BY N. F. R. SNYDER.

PLATE 7.

Common in the tropical rainforests of northern South America, the red-necked woodpecker (*Campephilus rubricollis*) is a close, but smaller, relative of the ivory-bill. Here a male pauses during a session of drums and double-raps at his nest entrance in a termite-infested snag of the Iwokrama Reserve in central Guyana in early 2008. In this location, as is true in many other Neotropical regions, *Campephilus* woodpeckers were more abundant than *Dryocopus* woodpeckers.

—PHOTO BY N. F. R. SNYDER.

PLATE 8.
Northern flickers (*Colaptes auratus*) regularly consume fruits of Coahuila junipers (*Juniperus erythrocarpa*) in Arizona. Like ivory-bills and many other woodpeckers, they eat substantial amounts of vegetable material and tend to feed most extensively on such food in late summer and fall. As a group, woodpeckers are more appropriately considered omnivores than insectivores.

—PHOTO BY N. F. R. SNYDER.

PLATE 9.
An ivory-bill roost hole in the Moa region of eastern Cuba in 1956 overlooked a broad expanse of cutover pine forest. Lumbering began in this region in the early 1940s and was scheduled for completion in 1960, but the revolution of 1959 temporarily interrupted operations before the very last mature trees were cut. Despite the extensive timbering, the ivory-bill, known locally as the "Carpintero Real," persisted in several cutover areas and did not completely disappear from the region until the late 1980s.

—PHOTO COURTESY OF GEORGE LAMB.

PLATE 10.

The only known photographic documentation of a living imperial woodpecker is 16 mm motion-picture footage of a lone female
taken in Durango in 1956 by William L. Rhein, a U.S. dentist.
Here, an enlarged single frame from this footage clearly illustrates
the white secondary feathers, white bill, and light-colored eye of
the species, although the bird's crest is not obviously recurved as
it is in other frames. Other portions of the footage illustrate the
same bird in flight, with her white wing feathers prominently
displayed. Although imperials were still being reported from
Durango into the early 1990s, Rhein's film and observations
constitute the last fully confirmed sightings of the species.

—PHOTO BY WILLIAM L. RHEIN, COURTESY OF MACAULAY LIBRARY AT
THE CORNELL LAB OF ORNITHOLOGY, ITHACA, NEW YORK.

PLATE 11.

Huichol villages grace the Sierra Bolaños of Jalisco today, just as they did in the 1830s when Gould's type specimens of the imperial woodpecker were evidently collected somewhere nearby. The Huicholes remain closely tied to their mountain fastness, where they continue to live as subsistence hunters and artisans off of the lands ceded to them, resisting attempts of outsiders to lease their lands for logging and grazing. Imperials disappeared from this region long ago despite the persistence of old-growth forests.

—PHOTO BY D. E. BROWN.

Cassin's Illustrations   Plate 48

The Great crested Woodpecker

On Stone by Wm E Hitchcock   Lith Printed & Col'd by J T Bowen, Phil

Dryotomus imperialis. (Gould)

PLATE 12.

This color portrait of an imperial woodpecker by W. E. Hitchcock appeared in John Cassin's *Illustrations of the birds of California, Texas, Oregon, British and Russian America* in 1856—a time when the species was still thought, erroneously, to occur within the boundaries of the United States. A stone lithograph, this portrait is believed to be the first accurate portrayal of an imperial woodpecker.

(a)

(b)

(c)

PLATE 13.

Study skins of a pair of imperial woodpeckers photographed at the Los Angeles County Museum (a) reveal the very similar body size of males and females, with males only slightly larger on average than females, but with considerable overlap. The most conspicuous differences between sexes involve the black, recurved crest of females (b), contrasting with the straight red crest of males (c). The ivory-white to pale-yellowish beaks of these 56 to 60 cm (22 to 24 in.) long birds range from 78.5 to 85.3 mm (3.1 to 3.4 in.) in length in males and from 72.5 to 84.7 mm (2.9 to 3.3 in.) in length in females (Winkler, Christie and Nurney 1995). As is the case with many specimens in U.S. collections, these two were collected in the vicinity of the Mormon colonies in Chihuahua prior to the Mexican revolution of the early twentieth century.

—PHOTO BY D. E. BROWN.

PLATE 14.
This mounted female imperial woodpecker was collected during E. W. Nelson's expedition in 1892. It is one of ten the party collected around the village of Nahuatzin in Michoacán. Subsequent expeditions were unable to relocate imperials in this region, as the area became densely inhabited by people in the early twentieth century and was extensively cleared for agriculture.

—PHOTO TAKEN AT THE U.S. NATIONAL MUSEUM BY K. B. CLARK.

PLATE 15.
The high-elevation forests of Cebadilla in the Tutuaca Reserve in southern Chihuahua, although not completely virgin, still contain some of the best near-old-growth stands in the Sierra Madre Occidental and the largest nesting population known for the thick-billed parrot (*Rhynchopsitta pachyrhyncha*). It is also one of the few locations for the endangered native spruce of the Sierra Madre (*Picea chihuahuana*). This was the location for which Plimpton (1977) obtained some of his most recent interview data for imperial woodpeckers, including reports of birds that had been shot for their feathers. But even though the region has been under intensive study by Mexican biologists in recent decades, there have been no more credible reports of imperials here.

—PHOTO BY N. F. R. SNYDER.

PLATE 16.

An adult eared quetzal (*Euptilotis neoxenus*) of 2002 arrives at its nest to provide a youngster with a praying mantis. The nest site is an old flicker hole in an aspen snag. During nesting, eared quetzals concentrate on mantids, katydids, moths, and other insects as food for their broods, but sometimes bring in small lizards. Like the imperial woodpecker, this species also takes much fruit in the summer, fall, and winter months. The eared quetzal, imperial woodpecker, and thick-billed parrot of high-elevation forests of the Sierra Madre Occidental, have all been considered threatened species, but the quetzal is less closely tied to conifer forests than the other two species and is most often found in riparian woodlands.

—PHOTO BY N. F. R. SNYDER.

PLATE 17.

E. A. Hankins III holds the painting of a trio of imperial woodpeckers by John O'Neill, which he commissioned in 1983 (see front cover of book). Hankins, the former curator of the World Museum of Natural History at La Sierra University (formerly Loma Linda University), is one of the few people alive today to have heard imperial woodpeckers, specifically a pair that evidently roosted adjacent to his campsite near Cueva del Toro, Chihuahua, in November 1972. In May 1981 he returned to the site and retrieved a section of a Chihuahua pine that he believed was likely the birds' nest tree.

—PHOTO BY K. B. CLARK.

PLATE 18.

The provenance of this mounted pair of imperial woodpeckers in the Bob Howard collection in Palm Springs, California, is unknown, but the birds are thought to have been collected somewhere in Chihuahua in 1907. Mounted imperial specimens are now rare and may number fewer than two dozen (appendix 2).

—PHOTO BY D. E. BROWN.

PLATE 19.

The montane conifer forest near El Salto, Durango, in March 1970 was dominated by yellow pines but also included mature madrones (*Arbutus xalapensis*), Douglas firs (*Pseudotsuga menziesii*), and Mexican white pines (*Pinus strobiformis*). The location is at an elevation of 8,700 feet and is not too distant

from where Walter Bishop, Arthur A. Allen, and William L. Rhein found imperial woodpeckers. The forest in 1970 was composed of mostly old-growth trees and showed little evidence of being logged, although commercial logging and settlement were underway. A recent wolf pelt was seen nailed to a forestry cabin. The last imperial woodpecker of record in this part of Durango was in 1956.

—PHOTO BY D. E. BROWN.

PLATE 20.

A Tarahumara village near Creel, Chihuahua, in May 1998 was occupied mostly by women and children as the men were working their fields of corn or hunting. On several trips to the Tarahumara country by DEB and KBC, no sign of game was noted. The only large tree-nesting birds observed were a flock of six thick-billed parrots thought to be passing through on their way north.

—PHOTO BY D. E. BROWN.

PLATE 21.

Guillermo Carrillo González, in native dress, flanks David E. Brown (left side of photo), Rod Dossey of San Diego (second from right), and Mike Perkinson (far right). Guillermo was our Huichol guide for a 2002 trip to virgin portions of the Sierra Bolaños.

—PHOTO BY K. B. CLARK.

PLATE 22.

Museum skins reveal size relationships among a Cuban ivory-bill male (*C. p. bairdi*) (far left), male and female ivory-bills from the mainland (*C. p. principalis*)(center), and male and female imperial woodpeckers (right). The total lengths of ivory-bills (range of 48–53 cm, or 19–21 in.) averages 13 percent less than imperials, while the wing length of ivory-bills (range of 236–263 mm, or 9.3–10.3 in.) averages approximately 19 percent less than imperials. The average length of the bill (59.5 mm, or 2.3 in.) of the only slightly smaller Cuban subspecies is 10 percent smaller than mainland ivory-bill beaks, which are 15 percent smaller than imperial beaks (Winkler, Christie, and Nurney 1995). Mean weights of freshly killed imperials are unknown but were probably significantly greater than the 450–570 grams (16–20 oz.) recorded for two mainland ivory-bills. In coloration, imperials and ivory-bills differ mainly in presence or absence of white stripes running up the neck to the head.

—PHOTO BY K. B. CLARK, COURTESY OF
THE UNITED STATES NATIONAL MUSEUM IN WASHINGTON DC.

PLATE 23.

A thick-billed parrot adult prepares to feed a nestling in a natural cavity of a Mexican white pine (*Pinus strobiformis*) snag in northern Chihuahua. Feeding mainly on conifer seeds, this species was a close habitat associate of the imperial woodpecker in former times. But despite a persistent folklore, the species has never been strongly dependent on imperial woodpeckers for nest-site creation, although it undoubtedly used old imperial nests on occasion in the past. Thick-bills nest in some regions, for example, the Sierra del Nido, where imperials have never been recorded, and today they often occupy old nests of flickers in addition to using cavities produced by natural decay processes, as seen here, often enlarging their interiors substantially with their strong bills. Presently considered endangered, thick-bill populations have been reasonably stable in recent decades.

—PHOTO BY N. F. R. SNYDER.

PLATE 24.

A petroglyph in a foothills canyon near Casas Grandes, Chihuahua, illustrates what clearly appears to be the head of a female imperial woodpecker. This figure may be the work of an artisan of the Casas Grandes Culture, which occupied the northernmost Sierra Madre Occidental from circa 1100 to 1350 CE. This culture was contiguous to, and contemporary with, the Mimbres and Mogollon cultures in adjacent New Mexico and Arizona.

—PHOTO BY N. F. R. SNYDER.

PLATE 25.

Hartweg pine (*Pinus hartwegii*) forest cloaks the east slopes of Cerro Potosí in the Sierra Madre Oriental. Why imperial woodpeckers have been historically absent from these pine forests in Neuvo Leon, Coahuila, and Tamaulipas, and from sweet-gum (*Liquidamber styraciflua*) and other cloud forest habitats in western Tamaulipas is puzzling, given the historical presence of ivory-billed woodpeckers in east Texas and imperial woodpeckers in the western portion of the transvolcanic range. Overexploitation by humans appears the most logical explanation for the absence of imperial woodpeckers in the eastern portions of the transvolcanic ranges, but this explanation may not be satisfactory for Nuevo Leon, Coahuila, and Tamaulipas.

—PHOTO BY D. E. BROWN.

PLATE 26.

Extensive ponderosa pine (*Pinus ponderosa*) forest in the Gila Wilderness of New Mexico has never been logged and is similar in general appearance and composition to former imperial woodpecker habitats in the northern Sierra Madre Occidental. Forests dominated by yellow pines, such as ponderosa, extend for nearly 500 km (300 mi.) from west of Williams, Arizona, eastward to west-central New Mexico, a region once touted by the U.S. Forest Service as the largest virgin ponderosa pine forest in the United States. That this region was historically without large woodpeckers, such as imperial and pileated woodpeckers, has long puzzled biologists.

—PHOTO BY D. E. BROWN.

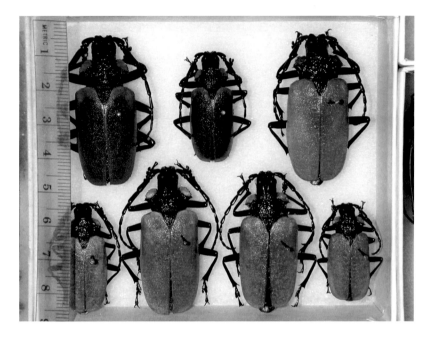

PLATE 27.

The cerambycid beetle (*Ergates spiculatus neomexicanus*) is associated with ponderosa pine forests and has a larva, popularly known as the *mesticui*. Up to 12.7 cm (5 in.) in length, this larva has been reported as an important food item for the imperial woodpecker. Another large species of long-horned beetle, *Oropyrodes maculicollis* (shown here), has a larva up to 17.7 cm (7 in.) long and 2.5 cm (1 in.) wide. This species has a distribution similar to the historical range of the imperial woodpecker and is associated with the Durango pine (*Pinus durangensis*).

—PHOTO BY FRANK HOVORE.

Chapter Two

LOST TREASURE
OF THE SIERRA MADRE

An Obituary for the Imperial Woodpecker

DAVID E. BROWN AND KEVIN B. CLARK

During a scouting expedition in the Apache campaign of last year Lieutenant H. C. Benson, of the U.S. Army, found this species to be common in the pine forests of the Sierra Madre, in Sonora, within fifty miles of the Arizona boundary. Owing to a lack of time and facilities he was unable to preserve specimens, but a head which he sent to the National Museum renders the identification of the species positive. This magnificent bird—the largest of all known Woodpeckers, considerably exceeding the Ivory-bill in size . . . will doubtless soon be added to the North American fauna.

—ROBERT RIDGWAY, *The imperial woodpecker*, 1887

Unfortunately, the "largest of all known woodpeckers" is now unlikely to be a member of any country's fauna. As is almost certainly the case with its smaller U.S. and Cuban ivory-billed relatives, this Mexican endemic is probably beyond saving. Yet, despite the existence of more than 160 imperial woodpeckers in museum collections, no one has ever maintained a live specimen in captivity, no eggs of the species have ever been preserved, and only a single live bird has ever been photographed (plate 10). We do not know when the last bird expired or even in what decade this occurred. How it was that this all came about in the twentieth century, when the concern for endangered species became widespread, is as fascinating as it is disturbing.

The written record of the imperial woodpecker began in 1832, the same year that Charles Darwin was aboard the H.M.S. Beagle, exploring the coast of Argentina. That year, John Gould, one of England's most avid ornithological collectors, was achieving another of his natural history coups. Laying a newly acquired series of specimens before an assembled audience of the Zoological Society of London, Gould had to have enjoyed a wry smile at the gasps of astonishment from the assembled naturalists. Among the birds on display were several striking black-and-white woodpeckers, each nearly 2 feet in length with generous 3- to 4-inch, ivory-like beaks. In a letter to Sir William Jardine dated December 19, 1833, Gould called the species "a complete giant" and sketched the head of a female with its curious black crest recurved toward its bill (Sauer 1998: 52). The crests of the males were more conservative in shape but were flaming crimson in color.

Pleased with his new acquisitions, Gould could not have foreseen the unfortunate fate of these birds, later dubbed *Campephilus imperialis* by the scientific community. What he probably did surmise, however, was that these largest of all woodpeckers would capture the fancy of a select cadre of royalty, scientists, naturalists, collectors, adventurers, and bird-watchers then participating in the major era of the description of new avian species around the world.

Probably collected by a mining engineer with whom Gould had an arrangement, the type specimens of these raven-sized birds were reportedly obtained in the Sierra Bolaños in the state of Jalisco in western Mexico. Extending south and east of the main Sierra Madre Occidental, the Sierra Bolaños rise to an elevation of more than 8,500 feet and support forests composed of several varieties of pines and evergreen oaks. Even today, the type locality for these immense woodpeckers remains much as it must have appeared in Gould's day, its forests uncut and sparsely inhabited by the native Huichol Indians (plate 11).

In 1836, another collector of ornithological treasures, Victor Messena, the duke of Rivoli, purchased an additional series of imperials (appendix 2). These specimens, the labels of which were removed prior to their acquisition by the Academy of Natural Sciences of Philadelphia, and hence of uncertain origin, may also have come from the Sierra Bolaños. What is known is that they were the last imperial woodpeckers to find their way into a museum collection for forty-six years, resulting in some confusion as to the actual location and distribution of these birds. Gould's birds were described as coming from the Pacific coast regions adjacent to California, and Cassin (1856), who was the first artist to illustrate an imperial woodpecker (plate 12), thought the species occurred in Mexico, California, Oregon, and possibly the southern Rockies of the United States. Indeed, the range of the imperial woodpecker remained uncertain (see Sclater and Salvin 1859; Baird, Cassin, and Lawrence 1860) until the publication of the annotated checklist by Salvin and Godman (1888–97), who on the basis of birds in the Heine collection described the bird as a Mexican endemic found in Sinaloa, Durango, and Jalisco. Even then the thinking was that this Mexican form of the ivory-billed woodpecker would also be found in the southwestern United States (Ridgway 1900; Coues 1903).

This confusion was due not only to the pine forest habitats of these birds being remote and isolated, but also to a series of political events that began with the Mexican-American War (1846–48) and continued on through the French occupation (1864–67), which made much of Mexico an unproductive if not outright dangerous locale for European and U.S. bird collectors. As far as Mexico's endemic "ivory-bill" was concerned, ornithologists and bird artists had to depend on a handful of collected specimens (appendix 2). Only after 1880, with a strong government in place and the subjugation of the Apaches and other indigenous groups, was it possible for collectors to systematically survey the pine forests of the high sierras of western Mexico.

It was at the beginning of this period, in late July or early August 1886, that H. C. Benson had the presence of mind in the midst of the campaign against Geronimo to collect an imperial woodpecker and send its head to R. R. Ridgway of the U.S. National Museum, thus becoming the first resident of the United States to collect one of these spectacular birds for science. There was a price to pay, however, as Benson, a resolute collector, was repeatedly chastised by his commanding officer for his youthful immaturity and audacity to travel alone through country frequented by Apaches (Wood 1970). Ridgway, for his part, determined that Benson's imperial had been collected within 50 miles of the U.S. border. In actuality, Benson's collection locale is more like 150 miles below the border, and the imperial woodpecker has never been reported from the United States.

The man principally responsible for making Mexico safe for travel was Porfirio Díaz, the country's president from 1876–80 and from 1884 until his exile to France in 1911 (Knight 1986). Although Díaz himself was a part Zapotec Indian from Oaxaca, he surrounded himself with European "*cientificos*" and strove mightily to modernize Mexico. He instituted an academy of science, complete with a scientific journal, and encouraged foreign technology in almost every section of the Mexican economy— much of it in the form of British and U.S. investment in railroads, mines, smelters, oil, ranching, and timbering. So taken was the Díaz regime with U.S. and European capital and know-how that he not only allowed U.S. and British citizens to take up large ranches and other holdings in Mexico's frontier, he also ceded several parcels of land in the then unin-habited northern Sierra Madre to the Mormon Church (Romney 1938).

The First Natural History Observations of Imperials

One of the first foreign naturalists permitted to explore Mexico in the 1890s was the Norwegian-born anthropologist Carl Lumholtz, who con-ducted an extensive survey of the peoples of the Sierra Madre Occidental during the winter of 1890–91 (fig. 13). Entering Mexico from the border city of Naco, Sonora, Lumholtz (1902) first saw imperial woodpeckers on the 8,900-foot Sierra de Nacori between the Rios Huehuerachi and Bavispe, an uninhabited locality that was to prove to be the northernmost record for the species and close to the site where Lieutenant Benson had collected the head of the one sent to the National Museum (Wood 1970). Lumholtz reported seeing these woodpeckers fairly frequently, at least at first, and noted that they occurred throughout the Sierra Madre Occiden-tal to as far south as Jalisco in the mountains north of the Rio Santiago. His winter observations, with snow on the ground and freezing nights, in the most northerly portion of the bird's range strongly imply that these woodpeckers were nonmigratory. Later, Lumholtz sent three imperials killed by an assistant (Figueroa) near the Mormon settlement of Colonia Pacheco to the American Museum of Natural History (appendix 2). These were followed by another eight specimens taken near Basaseachíc Falls and shipped from the railroad at Temosachic, Chihuahua, making Lumholtz the first naturalist to report on the bird in its natural habitat and forever linking the two together (J. A. Allen 1893; Vasquez 1996; also see fig. 14). After entering the domain of the Tarahumara Indians in the mountains of central and southern Chihuahua, Lumholtz (1902: 212) offered an explanation for the birds' increasing scarcity southward:

Carl Lumholtz (1851–1922) was a Norwegian explorer and ethnologist, who traveled the world in search of little-known indigenous cultures. He was especially fond of Mexico and spent many years there, with the support of the American Museum of Natural History. Perhaps his most famous exploration was of the Sierra Madre Occidental in 1890, which resulted in *Unknown Mexico*, a two-volume account published in 1902. A museum collector of the old school, Lumholtz made specimens of many of the imperial woodpeckers encountered on his journey, but he was also a meticulous writer and recorded much about the bird's behaviors and vulnerabilities prior to the arrival of nonindigenous peoples.

—PHOTO COURTESY OF AMERICAN MUSEUM OF NATURAL HISTORY RESEARCH LIBRARY.

The giant woodpecker is seen in the more remote parts, but it is on the point of being exterminated, because the Tarahumares consider his one or two young such a delicacy that they do not hesitate to cut down even large trees to get at their nests. The Mexicans shoot them because their plumage is thought to be beneficial to health. It is held close to the ears and the head in order to impart its supposed magnetism and keep out the maleficent effects of the wind. In the pairing season these birds keep up a chattering noise, which to my ears was far from disagreeable, but very irritating to a Mexican whom I employed. He used to shoot the birds because they annoyed him.

Lumholtz was not the only naturalist working south of the U.S. border. Between 1892 and 1906, E. W. Nelson (fig. 15) and his assistant E. A. Goldman conducted a natural history survey of Mexico for the U.S.

FIGURE 14.

Specimens, such as this mounted imperial photographed in natural surroundings in Mario Vasquez's 1996 book on Carl Lumholtz, continue to
crop up, and one wonders how many have been lost through negligence
or will remain forever unknown in private collections in Mexico and
the United States. Lumholtz believed the imperial was rapidly heading
toward extinction because of the depredations of rural Mexicans and
native Indians. Professional collectors accounted for at least 160 imperials, but such specimens, like the many specimens of ivory-bills, may
have represented only a tiny fraction of the numbers lost to depredations overall.

—PHOTO COURTESY OF ALEJANDRO ESPINOSA, MONTERREY, MEXICO.

Biological Survey that took them into every Mexican state and, on several occasions, into imperial woodpecker country (Goldman 1951). Nelson's first encounter with these giant woodpeckers took place in 1892 in the Montezuma pine forests of Michoacán near the Tarascán Indian settlements of Pátzcuaro and Nahuatzin. So intrigued was Nelson with these birds that he wrote what would be the only paper on the natural history of this species. Published in the *Auk* in 1898, Nelson's article described the imperial woodpecker's powerful physique, its open pine forest habitat, its breeding and nesting season (February–April), its proclivity for feeding in dead and dying pines, the shape and location of its nesting and roosting cavities, its rather slow, crow-like wing beats, its nasal "penny trumpet-like notes" (298) and other general behaviors. Nelson not only collected seven imperials on this trip but also closely observed living birds, including a wounded individual. Nelson was thus able to describe the birds' lemon yellow eyes, calling behavior, and tenacity for life, as well as how a young Tarascán, who had retrieved the only remaining egg of a pair from a nest for him, broke the precious cargo in a fall while rounding up livestock.

Nelson, who once ranched in Arizona's White Mountains, likened the imperial's Michoacán habitat to the ponderosa pine forests found on Arizona's Mogollon Rim and, like Ridgway, thought it probable that this species would also be found in Arizona one day. Although neither Lumholtz nor Nelson was able to determine the imperial's past and present distribution, it was through their publications and collections in the U.S. National Museum and the American Museum of Natural History that U.S. ornithologists and artists became fully aware of the species (Bendire 1895; Ridgway 1900; Coues 1903).

Nelson and the younger Goldman also collected other imperial woodpeckers near El Salto, Durango, and around the Mormon colonies in Chihuahua, but this species was never again reported from Michoacán. When Robert Lea and Ernest Edwards (1950: 161) revisited the Pátzcuaro-Nahuatzin area during the late winter and spring of 1947, they found the formerly extensive forests of Montezuma pine had been almost completely cleared for agriculture. Even the mountaintops contained only small areas of second-growth forest and, frustrated in their search for any remnant imperials, they concluded that the species "is undoubtedly absent at present from this section of its former range."

Although many U.S. entrepreneurs were active in the Sierra Madre

FIGURE 15.

Edward William Nelson (1855–1934) was one of the United States' foremost naturalists and ethnologists. After participating in a successful expedition to Alaska during the period 1877–1881, he honed his naturalist leanings in Arizona, becoming a special field agent with C. Hart Merriam's Division of Ornithology and Mammalogy in 1890. It was in this capacity that he and E. A. Goldman conducted a field survey of Mexico's flora and fauna, prior to Nelson becoming chief of the U.S. Biological Survey in 1916. He first came upon and briefly studied the imperial woodpecker in the state of Michoacán in 1892, and in 1898 he published the only detailed scientific paper ever produced on first-hand observations of the species' biology.

—PHOTO COURTESY OF THE ARCHIVES OF THE SMITHSONIAN INSTITUTION.

during Díaz's presidency, none was a keener observer of northern Mexico's wildlife than Charles Sheldon (fig. 16), who supervised the building of the El Paso–Chihuahua railroad in the 1890s. Spending his spare time hunting grizzlies and other big game in the then wild Sierra, Sheldon (1979: 149) was one of the few to appreciate the imperial woodpecker for totally aesthetic reasons, and he fondly reminisced about his experiences with these great birds:

> Frequently, giant imperial woodpeckers were seen, the largest of the family in the world, ever active, running up the pines or flying from one to another—their trumpet calls incessantly sounding. When in the woods who, when he sees a woodpecker, does not pause to observe it with peculiar interest? The sight of the large pileated in our northern forests is ever a cause for some

excitement. But imagine seeing from time to time all through the day woodpeckers twenty-two inches in length, with glossy blue-black bodies relieved by the white lower halves of the wings, and the long recurved red crests of the males and the black crests of the females!

The Major Era of Specimen Collecting (1890–1910)

The Díaz regime actively facilitated the founding and establishment of the Colonías Díaz, Pacheco, García, and Chuhuichupa in Chihuahua, and Oaxaca and Morelos in Sonora, as Mormons from the United States successfully colonized Mexico's frontier (Romney 1938). It was thus only natural that these settlements became headquarters for collecting expeditions, the U.S. mania for obtaining and cataloguing new species then reaching a peak. Several of the colonies were in or adjacent to the yellow pine forests favored by imperial woodpeckers, and these formerly hidden recesses of the Sierra Madre were soon visited by professional collectors such as Wilmot W. Brown and G. F. Breninger, seeking specimens for private collections or to sell to U.S. museums. Brown collected birds for John A. Thayer, for example, while M. A. Frazer collected for William Brewster (appendix 2). Some of the collectors, such as H. A. Cluff and H. H. Kimball were local hunters, hired to provide U.S. museums with study skins. Securing bird and mammal skins and guiding U.S. collectors became a cottage industry, not only for the entrepreneurial Mormons, but also for Indians and Mexicans living throughout the Sierra (see, e.g., Thayer 1906). The most prized species was the imperial woodpecker (Griscom 1933), and the value placed on its skin was such that more than 80 percent of the imperials in museum collections date to the 1890–1910 period (plate 13, 14; appendix 2). Given the popularity of egg collecting at that time, it is nothing short of amazing that no imperial eggs found their way into collections—or at least none that we know about.

During this period buying and selling wildlife specimens was big business in the United States, with several large dealerships acting as warehouses, acquiring and providing specimens across the country (Barrow 2000). For an upwardly mobile American during this Victorian age, stocking a private parlor full of unusual wildlife specimens was considered a sign of wealth and education. Many of the largest private collections eventually formed the nuclei of natural history museums. For

FIGURE 16.

Charles Sheldon (1867–1928) was one of America's foremost hunter-conservationists and was instrumental in creating Denali National Park in Alaska, establishing national wildlife refuges for pronghorn antelope, and fostering duck stamp legislation. While working as general manager for the Chihuahua and Pacific Railway between 1898 and 1904, Sheldon spent considerable time roaming Mexico's Sierra Madre Occidental, hunting grizzlies, deer, and other big game. His encounters with imperial woodpeckers during this period did not involve collecting and instead resulted in written descriptions of their aesthetic qualities.

—PHOTO COURTESY OF NEIL CARMONY, WILLIAM SHELDON, AND THE UNIVERSITY OF ALASKA AT FAIRBANKS.

instance Marshall Field, the Chicago department store magnate, purchased a sizeable collection from a large dealership for a hundred thousand dollars for display at the 1893 Columbian Exposition. This collection later became the basis of the Field Museum in Chicago (Barrow 2000).

One of the most prolific professional collectors of his day was Wilmot W. Brown, originally from Somerville, Massachusetts. By 1890 Brown had amassed an impressive collection of local birds (Hitchcock 1890), and by 1891 he was in the Caribbean, collecting birds in Puerto Rico and nearby islands (Cory 1892). In the late 1890s he moved out to

California, where his nephew, Chester Barlow, had co-founded the new Cooper Ornithological Club and was serving as editor of its journal the *Condor* (Swarth 1929). In 1897–1901 he traveled through Colombia and Panama collecting for Outram Bangs, who was later to become curator of mammals at Harvard's Museum of Comparative Zoology. Bangs (1899: 136), like many others, was amazed by Brown's persistence and fortitude, no matter what the conditions:

> Travelling in the Sierra Nevada [in Colombia] is at best slow and laborious and in the rainy season is harder still. Mr. Brown, in order to go as light as possible, carried no tent with him, and cut down his outfit in other ways till much too small for his comfort. Night after night he slept out with no shelter, wet to the skin by the terrific thunder storms that rage in these mountains nearly continuously throughout the spring. His one pair of shoes was soon worn out by the rough travelling, and for the greater part of the trip he went barefoot, his feet and legs exposed to the attacks of wood ticks and numerous insects with every now and then a narrow escape from a fer-de lance or a bushmaster.

Despite the difficult conditions, Brown sent over 1,000 bird skins and 350 mammal skins to Bangs after his first six months of effort (Bangs 1899). A few years later Brown left for Mexico in what would become a five-decade-long collecting effort throughout that country.

By 1906 he was collecting in Baja California, including a trip out to Guadalupe Island, where he collected the last Guadalupe storm petrels (*Oceanodroma macrodactyla*) and Guadalupe flickers (*Colaptes auratus rufipileus*) before those island specialties were finished off by the feral cats that had become established there (Thayer and Bangs 1908). His first experience with imperial woodpeckers came in 1905 in the Mormon colonies of western Chihuahua, where he took seventeen specimens in two weeks. He had apparently spoken of the value of the birds to well-heeled American collectors, and paying top dollar for specimens naturally led to excesses, as illustrated by this article in the March 1908 *Condor*:

> Recently there came to my knowledge facts relative to a deplorable slaughter of the Imperial Woodpecker (*Campephilus imperialis*), not so very far south of our border.

Two prospectors (one of whom imparted the information given herewith) were working over a region in west central Chihuahua some fifty miles west of Terrazas (pueblo), a mountainous and heavily forested country, much frequented by the bird in subject. One of the men had heard somewhere of the rarity of the species, and that it bore a commercial value, but erroneously, his conception was that the bill was the portion in demand, and not the prepared skin. Working on this idea he shot some seventeen of the magnificent creatures in the course of a few months, and cut off the bills, figuring them at $25.00 each, until on reaching civilization again, he was chagrined to find his material utterly worthless.[1] (Smith 1908: 91)

The End of the Collecting Era (1920–47)

In what could have been a merciful respite for the woodpecker, but evidently turned out otherwise, Mexico was embroiled in a brutal revolution that lasted from 1910 through the early 1920s (Brenner 1943). With the sierras in turmoil, the Saints, as the Mormons referred to themselves, were expelled, and most of the foreign entrepreneurs left the country (Romney 1938; Sonnichsen 1974). Taking their place were new arrivals: Mexican ranchers, poor settlers, and displaced Indians (Machado 1981). As new capital became available, logging operations gradually seeped into the pine country, replacing the concessions formerly held by U.S. and British owners. Populations of indigenous peoples, formerly absent from some areas and declining in others, greatly expanded. The old order broke down, and landless *campesinos*, woodcutters, and subsistence hunters roamed the countryside. Game laws were virtually nonexistent and .22 rifles and single-shot shotguns commonplace (Sheldon 1979). The effects of these changes on the imperial woodpecker, while largely undocumented, were undoubtedly less than propitious.

With the cessation of hostilities in the 1920s, Americans again began visiting northern Mexico's Sierra Madre Occidental. Included in this group once again was W. W. Brown, who now found the birds much more

---

1. These birds were not the same seventeen birds as those collected by Brown.

rare and again proceeded to purchase them from local hunters. L. A. Carlton (1922: 17; fig. 17), who kept a diary of his hunting trip into the sierra, revealed how high the price had risen:

> Saw giant woodpecker today. Rare bird and to be found only in these mountains. His coloring is gorgeous—blue-black, white and red. Very large. Perhaps twenty-four inches in length. The Whettens [J. A. Whetten was the party's Mormon guide] tell us that some museum or ornithologist recently procured a specimen here by paying $1500.00 for its capture.

The only specimens from the early 1920s are four obtained by Brown in the vicinity of Mound Valley, just south of the Mormon colony of Colonia Pacheco and now at the American Museum of Natural History. No bird could long survive with such a price on its head.

Nonetheless, despite fewer Americans coming to hunt, camp, and collect in the Sierra Madre after the revolution's end in 1922, those that did rarely passed up a chance to bag an imperial (Grimes 1928). Even today, diaries, mounts, and specimens of imperial woodpeckers being shot in the 1920s and 1930s continue to surface (S. Biggs, pers. comm. 2006; C. Rebar pers. comm. 2006). Some individuals, including a New York bank president, became obsessed with the idea of taking an "ivory-bill" as a specimen. Supposedly, after reading an advertisement in *Field and Stream* that an American named Swanson had "ivory-bills" on his Campo Bonito ranch in Chihuahua, he headed south immediately. Much to his wife's and employee's consternation, who hired a pilot to go down and warn him that *insurrectos* were about to take over the ranch near Laguna Babicora, he remained at Campo Bonito until "he had gotten him" (B. Williams 1984: 135). What happened to his specimen, like so many others, is unknown, but the last professional collector to obtain an imperial woodpecker was Chester R. Lamb, who took a male and female on July 28, 1947, south of Durango for the Moore Laboratory of Zoology in Los Angeles, California (appendix 2). His birds were not the last living imperials though, as evidenced by his notes accompanying the collected pair: "On top snag of a dead pine. 4 seen" (1947). This was just before the period of pervasive logging, which, while having begun during the Díaz administration, was poorly capitalized after the revolution until after the Lázaro Cárdenas administration (1934–40) and the stabilization of the

—"and thus equipped we took the trail"

FIGURE 17.
The relatively open pine forests of the Sierra Madre Occidental are visible in this photo of a pack trip near Colonia Pacheco, Chihuahua, in 1922. The tall grass is one of the mountain muhleys, probably bullgrass (*Muhlenbergia emerslyi*), a tropical grass that tends to disappear with heavy grazing. Fire frequency in the sierras is strongly related to the presence or absence of grass capable of supporting the spread of fires.
—PHOTO BY L. A. CARLTON, COURTESY OF RAUL VALDEZ.

political situation. Cárdenas and his successors were finally able to expropriate the last British and U.S. estates and apportioned out the lands to Mexican nationals, including to the native Indians (Brenner 1943).

Attempts to Find Imperials in the Mid- to Late Twentieth Century
By the time that the railroad passing Barranca del Cobre (Copper Canyon) bisected the Sierra Madre Occidental in the 1940s, the imperial was already a *rara avis*. Even in the still unlogged northern extensions

of the bird's range in Sonora and northern Chihuahua, several competent ornithologists working after World War II could report only old nest holes and recollections (see, e.g., van Rossem 1945; Marshall 1957). Nor were any imperials being reported from their former strongholds in the south in Michoacán, Jalisco, and Nayarit, where no birds had been found since June 1941 (Friedman, Griscom, and Moore 1957; appendix 2). The species was "now greatly reduced in numbers and considered in danger of extinction" (Miller et al. 1957: 44), and the few birds remaining were located mostly south of the railroad in the heart of the bird's range in southwestern Chihuahua and Durango, these states still containing some lightly populated areas within some of Mexico's best conifer forests. Areas within this region, as they became accessible, now became the primary destinations for those searching for the last imperials.

One of these searchers was a U.S. dentist named William L. Rhein, who located a pair of imperial woodpeckers in 1954 near La Guacamayita, Durango, where no one had seen any other imperials for the previous five years. Another trip to an area 80 miles northwest of Durango was unsuccessful, and Rhein then flew to a lumber camp in the Sierra de los Huicholes 80 miles south of Durango, where he was able to find only two trees with old roosting cavities at 9,200-feet elevation and the news that no one had seen a *pitoreál* (the Mexican name that literally means "royal pecker") for three years. On a return trip to La Guacamayita site he saw a lone bird and came upon an indigenous Mexican with a dead imperial, which he thought might have been one of the pair seen earlier.[2] This bird would prove to be the last verifiable account of an imperial woodpecker (Tanner 1964; Plimpton 1977).

Other ornithologists seeking to find imperials were R. L. Fleming and R. H. Baker (1963), who, together with a cadre of field assistants, searched unsuccessfully for these birds in western Durango in 1957. Although the bird was well known to local residents, who reported that this species had been sold as caged pets in the markets of Durango, the only actual evidence of the imperial's presence observed was the damage done to

---

2. One of these birds was captured on a 16 mm motion-picture film that was donated to Martjan Lammertink at the Cornell Laboratory of Ornithology, where it was made into a high-definition video (see plate 10).

trees by their workings and the nesting cavities in dead pines. At the time of their visit the only place reported to still have imperial woodpeckers was Rancho Las Margaritas southwest of Vicente Guerrero. Here, where wildlife was protected, the ranchers told them that the species could still be occasionally seen—usually in twos, sometimes four. Julio Carrillo, a local market hunter, told the team that the imperials were usually widely spaced, no more than one pair per large canyon, and that they flew high and for long distances. They were also told that dead trees were the main food source and were shown fresh workings attributable to imperials on Las Margaritas and on nearby timber lands belonging to the Indians. Large chunks of bark (up to 12 inches long) were knocked off of the dead trees where the birds fed on cerambycid (long-horned beetle) larvae (*Ergates spiculata*), known locally as *mesticui*.

On July 7, 1957, Baker (1958), in the company of Leslie C. Drew and John K. Greer, observed the felling of a large dead pine near Rancho Las Margaritas at 8,800-feet elevation. This tree, which was 80 feet high and 31 inches in diameter, contained a macaw nest (*Ara militaris*) about 60 feet up where the tree was 22 inches in diameter. The cavity was 6.5 inches tall, 11 inches wide and 29.5 inches deep. The nestling macaws were said to bring from Mex$25.00 to Mex$60.00 each, then between US$2.50 and US$5.00. The party was also informed that the cavity had originally been excavated by a pitoreál, as macaws were incapable of excavating their own nest cavity—a statement that was also said to be true for thick-billed parrots (*Rhynchopsitta pachyrhyncha*) (Bergtold 1906; Thayer 1906). In truth, the continued presence of both species of parrots reflects their abilities to enlarge nest holes made by flickers (*Colaptes auratus*) and other sources.

Another felled pine examined by the Fleming-Baker party was 25 inches in diameter and contained three nesting cavities, which were also about 60 feet up from the base, but attributed by their guides to having belonged to an imperial woodpecker. The largest cavity was 5 inches in diameter, 4 inches wide, and 13 inches deep. One of the guides stated that he once found two young in a nest in June and that the species also nested in large oaks. Unlike Lumholtz's birds, which appeared to persist throughout the year, the local imperials were said to favor the lower country during the winter months. All of the guides agreed that imperials were less abundant than formerly—both on the privately owned Las Margaritas and on the lands being logged by the Tepehuan Indians.

Carillo stated that the birds were shy and that a pair present in 1956 had moved out when a lumber camp moved in. All of the parties interviewed reported that the Indians did not kill the woodpeckers, and that the birds disappeared after the onset of logging operations and the felling of the dead pines.

Another searcher was Walter C. Bishop, who was to become the author of *Aves de Durango* (1998). Bishop's father was the U.S. vice consul in Durango prior to 1900, and he not only provided visiting Americans with information about the high sierra, he also knew and corresponded with such eminent naturalists as E. W. Nelson concerning various wildlife species. Young Walter was thus exposed to conversations about pitoreáles at an early age, distinctly remembering ornithologists coming to Durango about 1937 in search of the imperial woodpecker, supposedly on behalf of the Smithsonian Institution. Then, in 1939, as a young man working for a lumber company out of Hacienda de Coyotes, Walter himself came upon a group of five pitoreáles while on a hunting excursion near La Cueva—two adults, a juvenile, and two fledglings flying around a pine snag. Two years later, he saw a lone male in the San Juan Gorge about 2 kilometers down from the hot spring of the same name. These observations of duck-sized woodpeckers left a lasting impression on the youth, and he remembers the birds' unusual calls and tameness to this day (Bishop, pers. comm. 2004).

So fascinated did Walter Bishop become with pitoreáles that wherever his travels took him in his career as a lumberman and amateur ornithologist, he sought out any information that he could glean on imperial woodpeckers, hoping to get another sighting and gather some natural history data. Over a sixty-year period he queried loggers, hunters, campesinos—any rural informant that he came upon, as well as ornithologists such as Ceballos-Lascurain (1987) and Roger Otto (2003) as to the birds' whereabouts. But alas, although he interviewed men who had known and killed pitoreáles, none was able to show him a live bird. He received these reports with some frequency until the 1950s, but no one reported seeing a bird after about 1965. Walter Bishop (1998) regretfully concluded that the birds had succumbed to .22 rifles and increasingly invasive logging practices that involved settlements scattered throughout forests that had once contained trees 6 feet in diameter.

One man who came to photograph and study imperials rather than collect specimens was Arthur A. Allen, who arrived in El Progresso,

Durango, in mid-May 1946 to visit an area where Chester Lamb had seen one of the birds a few years earlier. On assignment with the National Geographic Society, Allen was experienced in locating woodpeckers, having pioneered with P. P. Kellogg the recording and playback of bird-calls, including those of the ivory-billed woodpecker. Allen (1951: 316) finally managed to glimpse an adult female imperial and hear it utter "calls like a tinny nuthatch" that were seemingly identical to those he had heard given by ivory-bills in Louisiana, but the potential nesting cavity he had located and staked out was unoccupied. He reported that the bird had been feeding on dead and decaying pines, including fallen logs, knocking off great patches of bark in the process of getting at the larvae underneath. His photographic and recording quests thwarted, Allen's main contribution was to verify that the imperial sounded much like a U.S. ivory-bill and to note that the bird's straight, duck-like flight carried it so far as to make it almost impossible to relocate. No one has ever recorded the imperial's call.

In 1962, James T. Tanner, who had studied the last known ivory-billed woodpecker population in the United States in the 1930s and 1940s, sought the imperial woodpecker in the mountains of southern Durango with even less success than Allen. Accompanied by his son, Tanner concentrated on the area where Rhein had found a pair in 1954 and seen a single bird in 1956, and was told that a few of the birds still persisted in the area. Although Tanner found an abundance of what he considered quality habitat, including nesting and roosting cavities, he found no pitoreáles. He was told of recent sightings (1961–62) in southern Chihuahua, southern and western Durango, and northeastern Nayarit, but the bird remained elusive. A letter to Tanner from F. K. Hinton (*in* Tanner 1964: 77) suggested why: "In southern Durango, around a new lumbering operation, the inhabitants claimed in 1953 to have shot 12 of the big woodpeckers within about a year." Unlike his 1942 assessment of the situation with the ivory-billed woodpecker in the southern United States, Tanner (1964) concluded that the imperial woodpecker was suffering not from habitat loss but from persecution, and he predicted that unless people stopped killing woodpeckers for food, medicinal remedies, and museum specimens, the bird was doomed to extinction. It is interesting to speculate what effect, if any, twenty years of reflection on the demise of the ivory-bill might have had on his conclusion.

The disappearance of so remarkable a bird would not be easily accepted, and a number of people have attempted to locate imperial woodpeckers since Tanner's visit. Many of these individuals were highly dedicated to their quest and more than one had a colorful personality. Each had a story to tell, and at least one of them probably saw an imperial.

The most infamous of these personalities was the late Ben Tinker: "game warden," hunting guide, self-styled naturalist, and author. At one time William T. Hornaday of the New York Zoological Society had paid a then young Ben Tinker to protect mountain sheep and pronghorn antelope along the U.S.-Mexican border. Tinker, for his part, spent a considerable amount of his time in the deserts of northern Mexico hunting pronghorn, bighorn, deer, and other big game animals—either for himself or as a guide for well-heeled clients. Claiming to have a ranch in the Sierra Madre, Tinker promoted himself as an expert on wildlife of the region and eventually wrote a book, *Mexican wilderness and wildlife* (1978), which was endorsed, with reservations, by A. Starker Leopold, a bona fide authority on the subject and the author of the prestigious *Wildlife of Mexico* (1959).

Unfortunately, Tinker claimed that he had seen white-tailed deer in Baja California, where this species does not exist, and claimed to have accurately weighed a variety of big game animals (including grizzlies) that he killed in remote areas. These and other improbabilities were not ignored by Leopold. Yet Leopold still believed that Tinker was someone that had truly seen imperials. In fact, Tinker claimed to have once photographed the species and to have shot one as a specimen and that both the specimen and photograph had been given to the Santa Barbara Natural History Museum, but unfortunately had been later lost in a fire. The museum in Santa Barbara had indeed been partially destroyed by a fire in 1962—so far so good—but when we contacted the museum and asked if any evidence remained concerning either the bird or its portrait, we learned that the museum's accession catalog, which had survived the fire, contained no mention of either an imperial woodpecker or Ben Tinker.

Tinker again surfaced as potential source of information when George Plimpton began work on an article on imperials for *Audubon Magazine* in the mid-1970s. Plimpton is probably best known as an irreverent New York editor and author of *Out of my league* and *Paper tiger*—books celebrating his hapless adventures attempting to replicate the challenging career experiences of famous personalities in sports and other endeavors. In 1976 he donned cut-off shorts and boots and ventured into the

Sierra Madre with two world-class bird-watchers, Victor Emanuel and John Rowlett, in hopes of spotting what was by then considered the rarest bird in North America. Plimpton's chief enabler was Victor Emanuel who immediately contacted Tinker on Leopold's advice and was informed that Tinker had seen an imperial somewhere in southern Chihuahua the previous year, although it was never possible to obtain accurate information on the location nor arrange for Tinker to serve as guide to the site. Beyond Tinker's nebulous claim, Emanuel knew the location of the sites in Durango visited by Rhein in the 1950s and had heard that a group of biology students had seen several pairs in the vicinity of Barranca del Cobre in 1973.

But when subsequent investigations failed to produce any corroboration of the latter report, Plimpton and his crew flew to the remote lumber town of Tutuaca in southern Chihuahua with Ike Russell, a well-known bush pilot who was familiar with the Sierra Madre. Here the party was informed that a pair of imperials had been seen only the previous year in nearby Cebadilla (plate 15), but on reaching Cebadilla they found no imperials, even though the magnificent forests of this location to this day still host impressive populations of both thick-billed parrots and eared quetzals (*Euptilotis neoxenus*; plate 16). Locals knew nothing of the imperials reported the previous year and informed the searchers that the last six pitoreáles in this region were killed for their feathers in 1970.

Plimpton and his companions also investigated other tantalizing rumors of the species obtained in other nearby towns and lumber camps, but all proved to be dead ends. Perhaps the closest they came to the species was when they interviewed a logging truck driver, who remembered a pitoreál that he had encountered fourteen years earlier (1962) as "*un gran pedazo de carne*" (one great piece of meat). Plimpton (1977) used this description as the title of his account of the expedition, and it is plain to see that as a skilled journalist marveling at the impressive forests still in existence in the region, he was not seduced by the argument that habitat destruction was the root cause of the imperial's disappearance. He clearly believed instead that the birds had simply been killed out by the campesinos that by then inhabited nearly all corners of the Sierra Madre Occidental.

Dr. E. A. (Bill) Hankins III (plate 17) may be the only living U.S. resident to have seen or heard an imperial woodpecker. Dr. Hankins is a practicing dermatologist and presides over an eclectic collection of mounted scarcities as the curator of vertebrate zoology at the World Museum of Natural History (WMNH) at La Sierra University in Riverside, California. This museum has an impressive display of mounted animals, ranging from passenger pigeons and ivory-billed woodpeckers to a Chinese alligator. Here, on a blustery February day in 2005, Dr. Hankins related to us how on a Thanksgiving-week trip in 1972, he, his wife at the time, and a photographer friend drove a Volkswagen camper bus to La Junta, Chihuahua, with the goal of eventually reaching the Barranca del Cobre. Leaving La Junta after dusk and pushing hard for the Barranca, the party proceeded southward on dirt roads for about 60 miles before stopping at around one in the morning to sleep in a pine-forested canyon at an elevation of about 8,000 feet.

In a pre-dawn sleep, Hankins dreamed that he heard the call of a pair of imperials. But as he awoke, he realized what he was experiencing was no dream, but a pair of imperials calling just outside. Hankins had listened to the tapes of ivory-billed woodpecker calls recorded in the 1930s and recognized that the calls were similar. The *keent-keent* notes of the pair calling back and forth penetrated into the camper where everyone else was still sleeping. It sounded as if the birds were in the trees close by, and Hankins woke the rest of his party to go in search. It was still dark at this point, the voices of the imperials resonating through the canyon that was otherwise deathly still except for the soft ripples of a nearby stream. On stepping out of the camper in the early chill, Hankins realized that the birds were not nearby but calling from the crest of the canyon wall some 500 feet to the east, and just out of sight.

As the dawn light gradually illuminated the canyon walls, Hankins and his party began to ascend the ridge in an effort to spot the calling birds. But such was not to be. The cries of the calling imperials became ever more distant until heard no more. Hankins marked the spot so that he could return later and continue the search.

Later that morning, about a mile from where the birds were heard, the party located a large snag containing probable imperial woodpecker nest holes in what was the largest pine tree that they had seen on the trip—a Chihuahua pine over 100 feet tall with a basal diameter of some 4 feet. After photographing the tree, and carefully noting its location for a return trip, the party went to a nearby Indian village called Cueva del Toro. Here, Hankins questioned the elders about imperials. Although some of them had seen the birds in the past, none had seen any in recent years. That night, a blizzard struck the Sierra, the worst in ten years, driving the Hankins party down to lower elevations.

In May 1981, Hankins and three others again made the trip south to continue his search. Although the nest tree was still standing, the local people had sawed through two thirds of the base in an attempt to fell the old monarch. Spending a couple of days at the site, the party took numerous photos of the tree from all angles. One member of the party was an experienced tree climber and, using professional climbing gear, ascended the tree up to the nest excavations, bagging up the contents he found at the bottom of the two cavities. Examination of the contents showed no evidence that imperials, or any other bird, had used the nest cavities in years.

Since nesting birds were no longer using the tree, and since it was in imminent danger of being toppled, Hankins decided to remove the trunk's upper portions to take back to the WMNH for display. On falling, however, the dying pine crashed down on the tops of lesser pines, hitting the ground with a thunderous roar among a humongous cloud of dust and debris. But even though the portion of the trunk containing the nest holes and cavities had broken into some two hundred pieces, Hankins and his party were able to locate every fragment, and painstakingly reassemble 26 feet of the snag and its limbs to haul back to California in the bed of a truck. That tree, partially reassembled, now stands in the preparation facilities of the WMNH (fig. 18), one of only two putative imperial nest cavities on display in the world—the other being at the Museum of Comparative Zoology at Harvard.

In 1983 Hankins commissioned Dr. John O'Neill, an ornithologist at Louisiana State University, and a world-renowned bird artist, to paint a pair of imperial woodpeckers. Using the nest tree photos provided by Hankins for his painting, O'Neill depicted two females on the snag of a Chihuahua pine while a life-size male dominates the foreground (cover portrait).

Hankins' friend and colleague, Bob Howard of Palm Springs, California, is another unusual personality involved with this now almost mythical Mexican woodpecker. Howard has spent his life amassing a collection of unusual animals that outpaces all but the largest museum collections. Walking through the front door of any one of Bob Howard's three houses is akin to entering a moribund wild kingdom. Here, if told where to look, one can find a full mounted okapi, an aardvark, and such extinct rarities as passenger pigeons, Carolina parakeets, and ivory-billed woodpeckers. Naturally, he has a pair of pitoreáles—purchased from a private collector who obtained them in Chihuahua who knows when. Having seen this species only as study skins, we must admit that upon seeing these well-prepared relics we were nearly as thrilled as if we had seen the birds when they were alive! (see plate 18).

There were also reports from Mexican biologists during the 1970s. At five in the afternoon on May 30, 1977, Alberto González-Romero saw a female imperial flying over the slopes of Mesa del Buro on the La Michilia preserve only a few miles from Rancho Las Margaritas. Two years later, on May 21, 1979, he saw a male perched on the Mesa proper in a *madroño* tree from which it flew rapidly (Gallina 1981). Both birds flew out of sight and were never seen again. A subsequent trip to Mesa del Buro by one of us (DEB) showed it to be populated mostly by evergreen oaks (*encinal*), with most of the ponderosa pines at higher elevations off of the preserve. In a March 2001 interview, Dr. González stated that he was positive about his observations, but believed that the circumstances were such that the birds were merely passing through, as all of his attempts to relocate them were unsuccessful. Although he believed "these woodpeckers are susceptible to forest harvesting and loss of dead trees," he considered these factors as only having accelerated the process of their extinction (pers. comm. in Jalapa, Mexico).

By the 1990s, the hope of finding a remnant population had pretty well faded, and the verdict of extinction had seeped into most conversations (Ceballos et al. 1992; Bishop 1998; Russell and Monson 1998). Not everyone agreed as to *why* the bird had become extinct, however. The International Council on Bird Preservation (Collar et al. 1992: 578) attributed the woes of the species fundamentally to "widespread modification of primary forest" and indicated that if the bird becomes extinct "this will be the overriding cause of its final destruction." Others, including ourselves, were (and still are) more inclined to believe that Tanner's (1964) prediction of loss of the imperial to shooting had come to fruition. Howell and Webb (1995: 765), in their definitive field guide to Mexican birds, covered both bases, stating that the bird's demise was "apparently due to hunting by humans for food, in combination with habitat loss." So which was the crucial limiting factor, hunting or logging?

With the passage of the Endangered Species Act in 1973, it was only natural that the U.S. Fish and Wildlife Service would take some interest

FIGURE 18.
This Chihuahua pine trunk, containing abandoned nest or roost holes potentially created by imperial woodpeckers, was retrieved in pieces by Bill Hankins in 1981. Reassembled, it is now located at La Sierra University. The two potential nesting cavities were 24 m (80 ft.) from the ground and nearly opposite each other. Both were located where the trunk had a circumference of 130 cm (40 in.). One entrance measured 11.4 cm (4.5 in.) by 12.7 cm (5 in.) and the other 12.7 cm (5 in.) by 15.2 cm (6 in.). The former cavity was 76.0 cm (30 in.) deep and the other 63.5 cm (25 in.) deep.

—PHOTO BY
DR. E. A. HANKINS III.

in learning if this endemic woodpecker from its southern neighbor might be still extant. In pursuit of this goal a number of cooperative expeditions and searches were funded by U.S. agencies and/or institutions in conjunction with the Mexican government. In the spring and summer of 1994, Ramiro Uranga-Thomas and Diana Venegas-Holguin (1995) conducted an intensive investigation to determine if the pitoreál still existed in southwestern Chihuahua. Concentrating in the best remaining habitats, the team made five field trips entailing more than 3,600 miles of travel to such places as Pino Gordo and Coloradas de la Vírgen in the municipo of Guadalupe y Calvo, and Corarechí in the municipo of Urique. Interviews with seventy rural residents, most of them elderly, were conducted in the bird's former range. Although they collected reports from eighteen people who claimed to have known the pitoreál, most of the observations had taken place many years earlier, and their conclusion was that the imperial woodpecker was no longer present. The reasons given were that the birds had been used for food and adornment, one individual even stating that the beak was used as pliers for extracting corn kernels. The natural history was as previously reported except that the imperials were said to spend some time on the ground and to raid the caches of acorns deposited by acorn woodpeckers (*Melanerpes formicivorus*).

Although a single bird had been reported seen in 1991, no sign of the bird's continuing presence was detected, and the last report of a credible sighting was about 1980, prior to any roads being present. Uranga-Thomas and Venegas-Holguin (1995) concluded that the bird had never been abundant within the memory of living people and that the main cause for the bird's extinction was hunting and deforestation—the latter not so much from logging as from forest fires, clearing for farms, and the building of roads and settlements. Two forest reserves were recommended to preserve the country's remaining biodiversity—a 56,833-acre area near Pino Gordo and a 157,650-acre block in the vicinity of Coloradas de la Vírgen.

The award for the most thorough search for an imperial woodpecker in this century has to go to Martjan Lammertink. A native of Holland and currently affiliated with the Cornell Laboratory of Ornithology, Lammertink made a 1994–96 survey of all of the old-growth forest haunts known to remain in the Sierra Madre Occidental (Lammertink et al. 1996; Lammertink and Otto 1997). Fascinated by large woodpeckers, Lammertink has also searched unsuccessfully for the ivory-billed woodpecker in Cuba (Lammertink and Estrada 1995), participated in evaluation of the reported reoccurrence of ivory-bills in the Pearl River Natural Area in Louisiana (Fitzpatrick 2002), conducted a study of the great slaty woodpecker in Indonesia (Lammertink 2004), and was most recently involved in the hunt for ivory-bills in Arkansas (Fitzpatrick et al. 2005).

Lammertink's search for imperials in the Sierra was habitat-based in that his mission was to survey old-growth forests to assess their status for endemic birds dependent on snags. To this end he began his nearly year-long field survey by first analyzing Landsat images superimposed on topographic maps and by interviewing Mexican forestry officials. Not considering canyon forests to be prime imperial habitat, Lammertink and his colleagues eventually visited most of the Sierra's summit areas above 6,600-feet elevation from Chihuahua to Jalisco. Here, he and his party searched on foot and horseback for birds and any sign of imperial woodpeckers, occasionally using ivory-billed calls in an attempt to elicit responses from any imperial woodpeckers that might be present.

In addition to inventorying old-growth forests, Lammertink and his team participated in sixty-two carefully conducted interviews with elderly inhabitants of former pitoreál habitat, some forty-eight of whom indicated that they had seen one of these birds at some time in their lives. Although most of the recollections dated to what Lammertink referred to as the extinction peak between 1946 and 1965 when there were still vast old-growth pine forests, fourteen respondents claimed to have seen an imperial since 1965, and a very few birds may have persisted into the early 1990s. "Convincing evidence" was obtained of a pair of imperials 4 miles north of Pielagos, Durango, in 1993 and signs attributable to imperial woodpeckers were found there in 1995. Sightings in 1990 and 1995 were also reported during a later survey of the Sierra Tabaco along the Sonora-Chihuahua border (Lammertink and Otto 1997). No birds were observed by Lammertink and his colleagues, however.

With respect to causes of decline, Lammertink et al. (1996: 33, 41) stated, "in some cases, logging and cutting of snags (which meant a sudden removal of all foraging and breeding sites) seems to have been the main cause of the local extinction of the bird. More often, before all old-growth and snags were logged, Imperial Woodpecker populations had been decimated by loggers and settlers who were armed with affordable .22 rifles. . . . The bird disappeared even before any logging had taken place in six out of 18 locations for which such information was available." Indeed, a majority (55 percent) of the residents interviewed by Lammertink et al. (1996) considered hunting to have been the cause of the bird's demise; only 29 percent attributed the bird's extinction to logging.

The reasons given for hunting the pitoreál by the twenty-three people who provided this information were interesting; 30 percent gave vandalism as the motivation. Other reasons were obtaining a novelty (25 percent), medicinal purposes (22 percent), and food (17 percent). One informant stated that all the males in an area of Durango had been killed for their red feathers. The feathers were said to be a cure for earaches, and the importance of this use was substantiated by one of the informants who still possessed the head of a bird that had been killed in the 1940s, but whose red crest feathers had been removed (Lammertink et al. 1996: plate 7).

Nevertheless, Lammertink et al. (1996: 1, 41) believed that habitat destruction would have ultimately wiped out the species if shooting had not already done so, and stated, "Recovery from the shooting became impossible through the ensuing logging of nearly all the pine-oak habitat." As a result, they considered extinction inevitable in that no adequate breeding and foraging habitat remained.

Yet when one views the mountains today, one sees no clearcuts and the slopes appear well forested with many mature trees. Certain species (e.g., Douglas fir, *Psuedotsuga menzesii*; white fir, *Abies concolor* and *durangensis*; spruce, *Picea chihuahuana*; and aspen, *Populus tremuloides*) are not cut at all, and large trees remain in some areas (plate 19). Snags can also still be found commonly in some regions, although cut for pulp in others. Just how pristine the forests might need to be to support the imperial has never been established, and Tanner's (1964) extremely conservative estimate of early imperial density (one pair per 10 square miles) prior to widespread timbering provides little insight into such matters. If the species might be able to tolerate habitat similar to that inhabited by the last Cuban ivory-bills (plate 9), there appears to be still a tremendous amount of habitat in the Sierra Madre Occidental adequate to support it. In any event the concept that the forests there might all be gone or massively degraded by logging is simply not true. The high-elevations forests remain well populated by trees and, although nearly all regions are subject to some cutting, the cutting is selective with no even-aged stands (fig. 19).

A great value of the survey conducted by Lammertink et al. (1996) was the inventory of remaining areas of forest not yet subjected to any mechanical logging. Of the Sierra Madre Occidental's original 36,124 square miles of pine-oak forest, only about 2,170 square miles were left completely uncut. Of this, less than 8.5 square miles were judged to be prime imperial woodpecker habitat. A series of reserves was therefore proposed, the most important being an area in the Sierra Bolaños, which today allows one to see what the bird's original habitat looked like in near-pristine condition.

In 2000 Jorge Nocedal, Miguel A. Cruz, Alberto Lafon, and Adolfo Navarro of the Institute of Ecology in Durango, Mexico, received a grant to survey the northern Sierra Madre for any reports of imperial woodpeckers. Although their survey efforts concentrated on isolated pine and pine-oak forest sites in the states of Chihuahua and Durango, these investigators also obtained reports from local people living in montane forests in Sonora, Zacatecas, and Jalisco. No old-growth forests were found, and Nocedal et al. (2005: 6) sadly concluded "that there is little chance that this magnificent bird may still roam the largest and widest mountain range in Mexico."

The most recent attempt to locate any remaining imperials was conducted by Sonoran Joint Venture, a Phoenix-based conservation program sponsored by the U.S. Fish and Wildlife Service to conserve cross-border wildlife. Hoping to check out possible sightings, the Service funded searches for imperials in northern Nayarit, southern Sinaloa, and Durango. Most of the areas visited were judged to be either unsuitable habitat or too dangerous to survey due to drug-trafficking (Beardmore, pers. comm. 2007). Needless to say, no evidence of an imperial woodpecker was obtained.

Still, unverified sightings continue, and perhaps always will. Ken Rosenberg relayed a sighting of a single imperial around the turn of the twenty-first century by two bird-watchers in old-growth forest south of Sierra Tabaco near the Sonora-Chihuahua boundary (Beardmore, pers. comm. 2007), where Lammertink reported a similar sighting in 1993. John Spencer (pers. comm. 2005) also reported an emeritus professor and his wife seeing a female imperial woodpecker in a pine tree from a distance of about 30 feet near Divisidero along the Barranca del Cobre railroad. According to the couple, they watched the bird for about two minutes before it flew off with a "raven-like flight." This was during the fall of 2005 at the height of the Brinkley hysteria over recent ivory-bill "sighting(s)." Subsequent investigations by several parties, including NFRS, turned up no imperials, and the only species found in the area that might have led to the report was the steller's jay (*Cyanocitta stelleri*), a crested species that under some conditions could be confused with a female *Campephilus*, given its shape and coloration. Although some nice yellow pines can be found around Divisidero, the number of Tarahumara settlements in the vicinity is such that a rarity as an imperial woodpecker would not have gone unnoticed (plate 20). Extraordinary reports require extraordinary proof, and the fact remains that a half century has passed with no verifiable record of a living imperial woodpecker.

We too have searched for imperial woodpeckers, although with neither Hankins's fortune nor Lammertink's fortitude. Beginning in March

FIGURE 19.

An aerial view of the Sierra Madre near the headwaters of the Rio Gavilán shows large pines and snags left after logging operations. Most of the logging had taken place on the ridges and bottoms, the pines on steep slopes of the canyons being lightly harvested or ignored.

—PHOTO TAKEN IN 2004 BY D. E. BROWN AND K. B. CLARK
FROM A LIGHT PLANE PILOTED BY SANDY LANHAM.

1970 and continuing on through the summer of 2002, one or both of us has made forays to those romantic places known to once have harbored pitoreáles—El Salto, La Michilía, and Rancho Las Margaritas in Durango; Babicora, Basaseachíc, Tutuaca, Creel, Pitoreál, and the Mormon colonies of Colonia Pacheco, Colonia Chuhuichupa, and Colonia García in Chihuahua; and the Sierra Huachinera along the Chihuahua-Sonora border. We also explored potentially promising sites adjacent to the Sierra proper—the yellow pine forests atop Cerro Guacamaya on the Chihuahua-Sonora border, the summits of the Sierras Catarina and del Nido in Chihuahua, and on Nevada de Colima in Jalisco—all places where the woodpeckers could have, or should have, been. Although these trips yielded sightings of thick-billed parrots, wild turkeys (*Meleagris gallopavo*) and various trogons, no imperial woodpeckers were ever seen or heard. What was worse, no one in any of these localities remembered anyone having seen a pitoreál after 1979 when Alberto González Romero reported a lone male on Mesa del Buro in La Michilía, Durango.

A Visit to the Type Locality for the Species

The Sierra de Bolaños lie in the state of Jalisco, north of the major Mexican city of Guadalajara. This sierra is slightly southeast of the main Sierra Madre, and far enough removed from major highways and urban centers to be rarely visited even by today's naturalists. Part of the reason for this lack of visitation is the fierce reputation of the local inhabitants, the Huichol Indians. A few years ago, a U.S. professor was killed while traveling through Huichol land. While the facts of that case are murky, and the blame may lie elsewhere than with the Huicholes, similar stories over the years are such that trips to the area are not taken cavalierly. Caution was very much on our minds as we left for a twelve-day sojourn to the Huichol country on August 2, 2002.

Bolaños is a charming colonial pueblo on the banks of its namesake river, with the towering sierra dominating views in all directions. As the final Mexican village on a dead-end road into the sierra, the town has a distinctively multicultural feel, with Huichol children in their native dress mingling freely with Levi-clad mestizos, walking the cobblestone streets below the imposing adobe church. Being the only U.S. tourists this place had seen in some time, we were quickly ushered into the alcalde's office, where we were received with gracious hospitality and introduced to the town's cultural liaison, Guillermo Carrillo González (plate 21). Guillermo is a Huichol, who not only speaks fluent Huichol, Spanish, and English, but also proved to be an invaluable guide to the sierra. After a day's stay in Bolaños to get resupplied, we struck out for the Sierra Bolaños with Guillermo, hoping to get a good look at pristine imperial habitat and a better understanding of why these birds had disappeared.

Entering into Huichol country with a multilingual guide was exactly what we had hoped to do, although the Huichol's reputation still gave us pause, and Guillermo's hat prominently displaying the letters EZLN did nothing to quell our anxieties. EZLN is the acronym for the Zapatista Army, a revolutionary militia force active in the state of Chiapas. The last thing we wanted was to be seen as partisans in a volatile region. But Guillermo came across as cheerful and more comfortable being a guide than a soldier, and with the mayor's assurances, we considered our bases covered as best as we could.

As we eased on up the dirt road into the sierra, the landscape changed from tropical thornscrub, to tropical deciduous forest, and then to pine-oak woodland. Finally, after an all-day drive, we camped near a ridge top at the end of a dirt spur road to a microwave tower at an elevation of 8,300 feet. The primary yellow pine here is the Michoacán pine, which differs from its ponderosa cousin in having a curved, less robust cone (Critchfield and Little 1966). Also present were the generally smaller Chihuahua pine and Lumholtz pine—the latter known as *pino triste* or "sad pine" for its drooping needles. As throughout the Sierra Madre, large oaks—ecological equivalents to Arizona's Gambel's oak—were important forest participants.

The biggest difference noted between this pine-oak forest and the ones we were familiar with in the U.S. Southwest was not in the composition of the forest, however, but in its structure (fig. 20). Owned and protected by the Huicholes, the forest floor had only recently been grazed by trespassing cattle and, as yet, only lightly. Clusters of young trees were scattered and few, and most of the forest was open enough to drive a team and wagon through. Old, dead, and dying trees appeared to be common and snags numerous and well distributed. Grasses covered the ground and orchids and other herbs were blooming in profusion. If any trees had ever been cut, it was too long ago for us to find any stumps or other evidence. All in all, it seemed to be ideal habitat for imperial woodpeckers, and the days we spent hiking and birding in the Sierra de Bolaños made us question whether habitat destruction had actually been the cause for their demise. But gone they were, "Nobody," Guillermo insisted, "had ever even seen or even heard of a pitoreál."

Piecing Together an Imperial Natural History

Perusing the bird collection in a large museum such as the Los Angeles County Museum is both exhilarating and disheartening. Inspecting the prepared skins of birds that we will never see in the wild provides a definite "rush," just as knowing that many of the locations given on specimen labels no longer exist as they once did is a definite "downer." These feelings are especially poignant when dealing with probably extinct species such as imperial and ivory-billed woodpeckers—birds now found

FIGURE 20.
Montezuma pine (*Pinus montezumae*) forest aspect in the Sierra Bolaños, Jalisco, is characterized by an open, herbaceous understory, widely spaced pines, and a general lack of small trees. The forest's open structure and tall canopy are maintained through inefficient or non-existent fire suppression practices coupled with a lack of commercial logging and low grazing pressure. The herbaceous understory allows for "creeping fires" that kill tree seedlings while sparing the large pines and oaks.

—PHOTO BY D. E. BROWN.

with certainty only in mothballed drawers (plate 22). What strikes us as especially saddening is that a life-history study of these birds is no longer possible—at least not one in the usual sense. Nonetheless, carefully documented specimens accompanied by good field notes can provide the rudiments of such a study when coupled with a little detective work (Remsen 1995).

Unlike the passenger pigeon, the last one of which expired in the Cincinnati Zoo in 1914, no living imperial woodpecker ever found its way into a zoological institution and the date of the last bird's demise is unknown. Were it not for literature records and the 160 or so specimens residing in the world's museums, one could almost argue that the bird never existed. But in truth, we actually know a fair amount about this species. As an example, the bird's distribution and habitat preferences are well documented. E. A. Goldman (1951: 192), who, like E. W. Nelson, knew the birds as well as anyone, had visited and collected specimens from Michoacán to Chihuahua, and described the imperial's habitat as "open pine forest with large pines [50 to 60 feet to the lowest limb] and many dead trees." The principal species were *Pinus durangensis, P. lutea, P. ayacahuite,* and *P. montezumae,* with trunks up to 30 inches in diameter at breast height. Nelson (1898), Lumholtz (1902), A. Smith (1908: 91), and others summarized the imperial's habitat as "mountainous and heavily forested country." Large yellow pines play an important role in all of the descriptions, as do some of the larger associated oaks.

All, or nearly all, of the accounts and collections come from pine forests in either the Sierra Madre Occidental proper or the western portions of the transvolcanic ranges in what biogeographers call the Madrean and Transvolcanic biotic regions (Goldman and Moore 1945). Moreover, most of the specimens were taken above 7,200-feet elevation in a yellow pine forest community within either Madrean Montane or Transvolcanic Montane Conifer Forest (Brown, Reichenbacher, and Franson 1998; map 2). The same holds true for Mexican geographic localities named "pitoreál" (table 2). All told, these biotic communities are relatively limited, only making up about 17,050 square miles in extent (Brown, Unmack, and Brennan 2007).

TABLE 2.
Geographic gazetter of pitoreál place names

19° 17′ N, 103° 11′ W	Place	Sierra Lalo, southwestern Jalisco	2000 m
25° 34′ N, 105° 56′ W	Village	Southern Durango.	2700 m
26° 23′ N, 106° 16′ W	Cerro	Chihuahua	2400 m
26° 35′ N, 107° 42′ W	Sierra	Cumbres del Caballos, Chihuahua	2400 m
27° 32′ N, 108° 01′ W	Place	Chihuahua	2400 m
27° 37′ N, 107° 46′ W	Rail Sta.	Chihuahua	2400 m
27° 37′ N, 107° 48′ W	Airstrip	Chihuahua	2400 m
27° 37′ N, 108° 13′ W	Cerro	Chihuahua	2000 m
27° 41′ N, 108° 12′ W	Place	Chihuahua/Sonora	2400 m

The collected specimens tell us that the sex ratios were close to one to one (appendix 2), and that imperials were almost certainly monogamous. The few juveniles in the collections also indicate that the birds had a low reproductive rate, as almost any imperial encountered was worth collecting. Breeding commenced in February, with nests excavated from 30 to 80 feet up in a large pine (Nelson 1898; Thayer 1906; Fleming and Baker 1963). And, although courtship rituals were never observed, the animated antics reported for ivory-billed woodpeckers during nest exchanges (Allen and Kellogg 1937; Tanner 1942), suggest that the imperial male's red crest and contrasting black-and-white wing pattern would have produced a truly spectacular show. The clutch of the related ivory-billed woodpecker of the southeast United States and Cuba averaged three eggs per clutch, and an informant told Lammertink et al. (1996) that some imperial broods contained three young, but Nelson (1898), Tanner (1942), and Fleming and Baker (1963) reported a clutch size of only two in imperials.

Judging from Tanner's ivory-bill observations, male and female imperials probably shared incubation duties, with males normally incubating at night. Eggs probably hatched in about twenty days, and nestlings probably reached fledging age in five to six weeks. The first fledglings were reportedly seen in April, with most youngsters likely leaving the nest in May or early June, as the three juveniles that we found in collections with the dates recorded were all taken in June and July. Parental investment probably did not cease with fledglings, as large, noisy groups of imperials, some consisting of up to ten individuals, were regularly reported between the months of June and January (e.g., Nelson 1898; C. Lamb 1947; appendix 2). Such gatherings, while not necessarily composed of closely related individuals, must often have included more than a pair and their young of the year, and may sometimes have also included offspring from the previous year. If so, it would be reasonable to hypothesize that the young required an extended adolescence, the immature birds possibly assisting their parents with the next brood and not breeding until their second year.

Tanner (1942) also speculated that ivory-bills may not have regularly bred until their second year, and he reported an instance of a year-old male still traveling to some extent with his parents as they conducted a subsequent breeding attempt. Nonetheless, Tanner believed that young ivory-bills often separated from their parents during their first winter, and it seems clear that they rarely associated in groups larger than parents together with recently fledged young, while imperials often associated in larger groups (see Nelson 1898; Tanner 1942; Lammertink et al. 1996). The ecologically similar Magellanic woodpecker (*Campephilus magellanicus*) that inhabits southern beech forests of Chile and Argentina also exhibits extended adolescence, with young birds sometimes remaining in family groups for two years or more before breeding (Ojeda 2004).

No direct data exists on nestling diet, but it is a reasonable speculation that this species, like the ivory-bill, relied mostly on insects such as various beetle larvae during the breeding season. Nevertheless, two paired birds collected during the early breeding season (February) were found to have "piñon berries" in their stomachs, likely referring to the large rich seeds of piñon pines (Gaut 1904). Imperials were also observed to have raided acorn woodpecker granary trees for acorns (Uranga-Thomas and Venegas-Holguin 1995), much as McIlhenny (*in* Bendire 1895) reported ivory-bills raiding squirrel nests for acorns. The number of times this behavior was mentioned by observers implies that it was a regular occurrence, and it seems likely that the imperial was a highly omnivorous species, with feeding habits similar to those of the ivory-bill and other *Campephilus* woodpeckers overall. The better studied Magellanic woodpecker of Patagonia, while feeding commonly on wood-boring larvae, has also been reported feeding on fruit, small vertebrates, avian eggs and nestlings, and even drilling and maintaining sap wells (Ojeda 2003; Ojeda and Chazarreta 2006; Schlatter and Vergara 2005).

Determining historical population densities and sizes is much more problematic. Some accounts suggested that the bird was relatively common in early times (e.g., Nelson 1898; Lumholtz 1902; Bergtold 1906; Goldman 1951), but none of these reports gave quantitative information on population densities. However, it is noteworthy that most such reports came from areas either just beginning to be exploited by mestizos or where indigenous Indians were absent or present in low densities.

The most detailed early report was that of Nelson (1898), who noted that local Indians reported imperials to be still "common" in some locations. Nelson found twenty to twenty-two imperials along his route of travel— a route extending roughly 25 miles—but he did not specify how much area he may have covered on his journey. Thus, there is no way to accurately calculate a density of the species on the basis of his report. Despite such limitations, Tanner offered tenuous speculations that Nelson's data could be interpreted to imply eighteen individuals in some 90 square miles (or one pair per 10 square miles). But if one applies Tanner's own data on vocal detectability of ivory-bills to the imperial (i.e., birds audible from one quarter mile and vocalizing about half the daylight hours), and assumes that Nelson did not wander widely from his described route, a density as high as nearly one pair per square mile could be calculated. Moreover, Nelson observed an imperial population that may already have been depleted by humans, as he described local inhabitants, a village, and corn fields as being present in the region, so there is no reason to believe that Tanner's density figure, or even a figure ten times as great, might represent a maximum or original density of the species.

Also questionable is the estimate by Lammertink et al. (1996) of a total original population of only eight thousand individuals, based on Tanner's (1964) density estimate for the species and an estimate of roughly 40,000 square miles of pine-oak habitat originally available. As just considered, Nelson's (1898) observations do not rule out an imperial population ten times as dense as calculated by Tanner, which would translate to a total population ten times as large as the estimate of Lammertink et al., not even taking into account that imperial numbers may already have been significantly depleted by human depredations at the time of Nelson's observations. Suffice it to say, that given the substantial populations of people historically present in imperial range, the number of imperial woodpeckers in Mexico a century ago was probably far below pristine levels and could have been similar to, or even less than, the depressed number of ivory-bills left in the United States at the same time. There is no reason to assume that either of these species was at carrying capacity of food resources during this period.

Chronology and Causes of Decline

Another intriguing aspect of the museum collections is the chronology of the birds collected (appendix 2). Generally, the collection sequence began in the south and progressed northward (map 2). As recently as April 1941, Kelly Simmons, living in Chihuahua, wrote Tanner (1942: 101) that imperial woodpeckers "were easily found, although not common, in the high pine timber at an altitude of from 7500 to 9000 feet along the Sonora-Chihuahua line." By this time it had been several decades since birds had been seen or collected in Michoacán. This progression northward, we believe, was no accident of collector interest, but a measurement of human settlement and persecution. Simply put, the imperial woodpeckers first disappeared from those areas having a dense indigenous population, and persisted longest in those areas within the *despoblado* region—the country abandoned by the Casas Grandes culture in the fourteenth century and not settled again until the arrival of the Mormons in the 1890s (Di Peso 1974). That the bird persisted longest in southern Durango and northern Chihuahua is consistent with the fact that these areas were densely settled only in relatively recent times, the number of *ejidos* (rural communities) more than doubling between 1930 and 1960 (Machado 1981). In addition, Fleming and Baker (1963), who visited Durango in the 1950s, noted that the Tepehuanes may not have hunted the species as extensively as did other indigenous peoples.

Thus, it was that the final few birds were taken in the northern center of the species' range, the imperial woodpecker surviving longest in Durango, where the bird was ultimately exterminated by collectors and logging-settlement inhabitants intent on hunting it for food and supposed medicinal values. We agree with Tanner (1964: 79), who stated, "while at first I believed that logging of the pine forest was the primary cause of the disappearance of the Imperial Woodpecker, my observations in Durango have convinced me that shooting by man is the chief cause of its elimination." Not only were the birds highly desirable from a culinary and medicinal standpoint, but they also possessed characteristics that led to their easy destruction so that they were highly susceptible to overhunting by both indigenous and modern cultures.

All accounts describe imperials as being not only large and conspicuous, but noisy, and habitually found during the fall and winter in groups of two to ten. Early naturalists such as E. W. Nelson (1898: 220) observed that these birds were "surprisingly easy to stalk, even after being hunted and shot at for several days." As he further explained, pitoreáles did not tend to fly away when one was fired upon, as "They showed considerable attachment to one another and when one was shot the other members of the flock remained scattered about on the trees for a short time calling each other at intervals."

Tanner's observation in the early 1960s that apparently ample good habitat still remained for these woodpeckers in the Sierra Madre remains our assessment today. But wanting to check out our ground observations from the air, we engaged Sandy Lanham to fly us over the highest portions of the sierra along the Chihuahua-Sonora border on December 12 and 13, 2004. This flight confirmed our impressions from the ground: large trees and snags were not in obvious short supply. Although the Mexicans log nearly all pine forests on flat terrain and modest slopes, the loggers typically "high grade" the most valuable and accessible trees, leaving much of the canyon forests relatively intact. This practice reduces the eventual number of snags in the forest by removing trees before the end of their life cycle, but snag losses due to logging are at least partially compensated by snag production resulting from the high frequency of lightning strikes (Douglas et al. 1993). The 10,000–foot peaks of these mountains are situated above a semitropical region adjacent to a warm-water coast that generates intense thunderstorms every summer, the resulting lightning igniting small fires on the ridgelines that often burn 5 to 100 acres of forest at one time.

Our earlier ground observations of the high quality of imperial wood-pecker habitat in the Sierra de Bolaños and elsewhere were borne out by these aerial observations and strongly support a conclusion that lack of enough properly forested habitat was not the primary cause of the extinction of the imperial woodpecker, much as George Plimpton had concluded earlier. Sustenance hunting for meat and cultural accouter-ments by local peoples was much more plausible as the main driving force—a general pressure causing scarcity and extinctions not only in the Sierra Madre, but throughout much of the U.S. Southwest and the world over (Bennett and Zingg 1935; Taylor and Albert 1999; Fa, Currie, and Meeuwig 2003). Game animals, including deer, black bear, and even tree squirrels are now rare throughout the Sierra Madre Occidental (Leopold 1959; Carmony and Brown 1983), while grizzly bears and wolves have been totally extirpated (Brown 1983, 1985b). The imperial was one of the most vulnerable species. In addition to being desirable as a food item because of its size (potentially greater than 1.5 pounds), it was highly visible and approachable and was relentlessly pursued as a species of medicinal value. It further represented a tremendous amount of money for rural people when sold to specimen collectors. Hence, it wasn't log-ging per se, but the loggers and their families that likely eliminated the last vestiges of these treasures of the Sierra Madre.

Nevertheless, other factors undoubtedly contributed to the imperial's extermination. Unlike the also snag-requiring thick-billed parrot, which survives in fair numbers in the Sierra Madre today (plate 23), imperials appear to have migrated only locally if at all (Lumholtz 1902; Fleming and Baker 1963). Nor did they readily colonize new areas. We know of no records of imperials ever inhabiting or visiting suitable-appearing pine forests in outlying ranges such as the Sierra del Nido, Sierra de las

Tunas, and Sierra Catarina. Thus the species may have had little capacity to respond to local stress by leaving to go elsewhere.

In contrast, thick-billed parrots are known to have nested in the Sierra del Nido and to have sometimes visited mountain ranges in the southwestern United States in substantial numbers during periods of food stress in Mexico in the early twentieth century (Snyder, Enkerlin-Hoeflich, and Cruz-Nieto 1999). Moreover, the thick-bill also has a close relative, the maroon-fronted parrot (*Rhynchopsitta terrisi*) that occupies and exploits the pine forests of the Sierra Madre Oriental of eastern Mexico, a region never known to be frequented by the imperial woodpecker or any other *Campephilus* species, contemporary or fossil, despite the apparent suitability of habitat there. Could the vulnerability of the imperial in part be a reflection of apparently sedentary habits? The limited historical range of the imperial appears consistent with this suggestion.

This explanation could also help answer another distribution question—one raised by Robert Ridgway's erroneous speculations on the range of the species that serve to introduce this chapter. Why was the imperial historically absent from the great ponderosa pine forests of Arizona and New Mexico? These forests, recently celebrated as the finest virgin stands of ponderosa pine in the world, would appear to have been ripe for the taking by these woodpeckers since the late Holocene. Yet there are no records, recent or fossil, of the species' presence in these forests in spite of the occurrence of an extinct relative, *Campephilus dalquesti*, in west-central Texas two million years ago (Brodkorb 1971). Could this simply have been due to limited dispersal abilities in the imperial?

Although this hypothesis is difficult to rule out, we are hesitant to believe that it provides an adequate explanation, in part because the pine forests of central Arizona and New Mexico are so proximate to the Sierra Madre Occidental and nearly connected by Madrean evergreen woodland and montane forest sky-islands in southeastern Arizona and southwestern New Mexico. The distances between seemingly good patches of habitat are simply too small to be convincing barriers for a strong-flying species, given the lengths of time involved. The ancestors of *Campephilus imperialis* must have persisted through many fluctuations in climate and vegetation patterns, suggesting that the modern distribution of the imperial woodpecker may not be due solely to a reluctance to fly across unfavorable habitats but also to past isolations and disappearances. No pileated (*Dryocopus pileatus*) or other large woodpeckers were present in Arizona or New Mexico to compete with any imperials that flew a distance of less than 100 miles from occupied ranges in northern Chihuahua and Sonora to take up residency in the forested Chiricahua, Huachuca, Animas, and other southern Arizona and New Mexican mountain ranges. These mountain ranges are visible from the tops of the northernmost ridges of the Sierra Madre in clear weather and represent a flight of no more than a couple hours duration across the intervening grasslands and desert.

Another factor potentially limiting past distribution of the imperial is human exploitation. This hypothesis too has its problems, as it would seem to require a more pernicious use of woodpeckers north of the border in early times than farther south. The Pueblo Indians of the U.S. Southwest certainly used bird feathers in their ceremonies, and some Indians such as the Zuni still do (Taylor and Albert 1999). But although the use of birds and bird feathers by indigenous peoples in Arizona and New Mexico is well documented, and some kiva murals depict birds reminiscent of imperial woodpeckers (W. Smith 1952; Hibben 1975; fig. 21), archaeologists have yet to find any remains of *Campephilus imperialis* in the U.S. Southwest (Hargrave 1939; Phillips, Marshall, and Monson 1964). And if the mural depictions were of imperial woodpeckers, they could have represented trade items brought from Mexico, as was the case with the macaws (*Ara macao*) found in the pueblos prior to their great abandonment between 1350 and 1450 CE (Di Peso 1974). A petroglyph (plate 24) near Casas Grandes, Chihuahua, is unmistakably a female imperial woodpecker. But, even if the great birds had been extirpated during Anasazi times, there would seemingly have been plenty of opportunity to have recolonized the "despoblado" during the past five hundred years. Early cultural exploitation might well explain the imperial's historical absence from the pine forests of Mexico's transvolcanic ranges and Sierra Madre Oriental (plate 25), but seem less convincing as an explanation for the bird's absence from the extensive pine forests of the Pinaleño Mountains, the North Kaibab, and Mogollon Rim (plate 26).

What other forces might have served to set the northern limits of the imperial's range? This is a most difficult question to answer. The possibilities range from geographic trends in climate and food supplies to changes in stresses from predation, parasites, or disease. The factors controlling range limits have been established for very few bird species. The distribution and abundance of such a supposedly preferred food item as

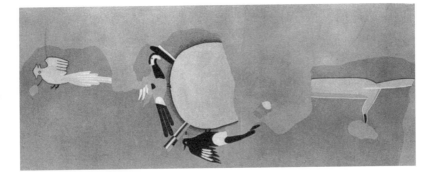

FIGURE 21.

An Anasazi mural at the Awotovi ruins dated at circa 1420 CE depicts a bird that could be an imperfect representation of an imperial wood-pecker (see fig. 5ba in Smith 1952). Other kivas on the present-day Hopi and Navajo Indian reservations contain similar representations, along with those of Mexican parrots and raptors, and one wonders if these figures were drawn from memories of these birds in Mexico, if these species once occurred in the wild in areas north of the border, or if they represented trade items, as was surely the case with scarlet macaws (*Ara macao*). Parrot remains have been recorded from a number of Native American middens within the United States, but no remains of imperial woodpeckers have ever been found in such sites. Watson Smith, *Kiva Mural Decorations at Awatovi and Kawaika-a with a Survey of Other Wall Paintings in the Pueblo Southwest*, Papers of the Peabody Museum of American Archaeology and Ethnology, vol. 37.

the mesticui might provide such a possibility except that this particu-lar cerambycid species does extend northward into the pine forests of Arizona and New Mexico (F. Hovore, pers. comm. 2004).

Another "lunker" larva, *Oropyrodes maculicollis*, appears to be a some-what better fit. This species has a grub exceeding up to 7 inches in length (plate 27) and occurs primarily in forests containing Durango pine (*Pinus durangensis*), a yellow pine closely related to ponderosa pine and having a distributional range coinciding almost exactly with the former range of *Campephilus imperialis* (F. Hovore, pers. comm 2004; Critchfield and Little 1966). Could it be that the bird's presence was determined by the distribution of a particular tree and the food it provided? This is unlikely, however, as there is no reason to suggest that the imperial woodpecker was a food specialist, and such biogeographical comparisons may be merely clues to larger phenomena than cause and effect. The lack of imperial woodpeckers in Arizona and New Mexico may be due to an as yet unknown factor or factors that determine the distribution of both *Pinus durangensis* and *Campephilus imperialis*. Or, it may be that the ponderosa pine forests of Arizona and New Mexico were too new to acquire a full complement of Madrean flora and fauna, having only recently becoming established in the U.S. Southwest during Holocene times (see e.g., Betancourt 1990).

Whether these or any other hypotheses have any merit we now have no way of testing. What is worse, we now know that we almost surely will never see or hear an imperial woodpecker, much less study one. As Guillermo said, "the times were not favorable for such a bird's survival." The age of the pitoreál appears to have come and gone.

Chapter Three

OVERVIEW
AND CONSERVATION

The explanations proposed for the declines of endangered species sometimes achieve widespread acceptance without anyone ever thoroughly testing their validity against alternative explanations. Yet the consequences of misidentifying causes of decline can be severe and irreversible. Species can sometimes be lost by a failure of conservation efforts to address important limiting factors, and large sums of money can be expended unnecessarily correcting factors that are not crucial to recovery. Correct identification of the factors that are important in producing population declines is usually a prerequisite for success in recovery efforts.

For well over a half century, the intensive studies conducted by James Tanner have served as the primary source of knowledge for discussions of the biology and conservation of the ivory-billed woodpecker. By extension, many of the characteristics of the ivory-bill put forth by Tanner have also been assumed to apply to the closely-related imperial woodpecker, a species that was never studied intensively by anyone, but whose decline closely matched that of the ivory-bill in timing. Not all recent authors writing about these two species have advocated exactly the same conclusions, but a general consensus viewpoint has emerged that underlies almost all conservation recommendations offered to date for these species.

Two important components of this consensus are (1) an assumption that because of highly specialized feeding habits both woodpecker species were always rare, even in early times, and (2) an assumption that individuals of both species required huge expanses of pristine woodlands to obtain sufficient food. As so portrayed, these species have become powerful symbols of the original virgin forests of the continent, and, in popular view, their endangerment and potential extinction appear to have been all but guaranteed by their sensitivity and vulnerability to the declines in food supplies caused by widespread logging.

In many respects, available data from the last known populations of these species and early analyses of these data are consistent with these concepts. The ivory-bill fed by apparently specialized bark stripping in over 70 percent of Tanner's direct observations, and the final disappearance of many ivory-bill populations evidently correlated closely in time with the initiation of logging. The ivory-bill population studied by Tanner in Louisiana was indeed very thinly spread in its virgin forest habitat—only one pair per 17 square miles—and Tanner calculated from the data of early specimen collectors that the maximum density of this species was only about one pair per 6 square miles, an area that was matched in size by the foraging range he documented in one pair under close study. For the imperial woodpecker, Tanner estimated a quite similar figure of one pair per 10 square miles from observations made by Nelson in Michoacán—very close to what one might expect, by comparison, for a slightly larger bird. These estimates and projections all seemed in harmony with a view that these were food-limited species that simply could not tolerate much degradation of their forested habitats, although in the case of the imperial woodpecker in Durango, Tanner believed that Mexican timbering practices were sufficiently light and selective that the last imperials were extirpated mainly by hunting.

Nevertheless, as we have examined in the preceding two chapters, there are some troubling problems with these concepts and conclusions—especially stemming from the substantial number of apparently independent historical accounts claiming that these species were once common to abundant. Indeed, no one has ever presented a detailed analysis of historical reports that persuasively demonstrates widespread rarity of either species in early times. Yet without such a demonstration, the food-specialization hypothesis loses much of its plausibility. In essence, if ivory-bills and imperials were indeed once relatively common, as early reports quite consistently claim, there is no compelling reason to believe that they were extreme food specialists dependent on huge areas of forest, or that their disappearance was linked primarily to the declines in food supplies caused by the lumbering of virgin forests.

A close examination of historical information suggests that Tanner may have substantially underestimated early densities of both species and overestimated their requirements for forested habitats, in part by not recognizing that their diets were really quite generalized, and in part by not recognizing that the foraging ranges of adjacent pairs may have overlapped extensively. Early abundance reports and comparisons with other closely related woodpeckers suggest that regional densities for both species may well have reached several pairs per square mile in good habitat, while observations of early naturalists suggest that both species used a variety of foraging techniques and took many kinds of foods, including much plant material—not clearly the sort of diet demanding huge areas of forest. In fact, early accounts give no clear evidence that these species were generally food limited, and instead the common theme repeated over and over in these accounts is just how much both species were suffering from human depredations, especially because of their edibility, their values as specimens and trophies, and their high vulnerability resulting from their approachability, their tendency to vocalize steadily for long periods, and their tendency to remain in close proximity to fallen comrades. The last mentioned trait also represented a major weakness for the Carolina parakeet—see Snyder (2004).

What we favor from the examination of numerous early accounts of these species is an alternative explanation for their demise that is admittedly much less inspiring than Tanner's emphasis on their potential needs for pristine habitat, but that appears to fit historical facts much more closely. It appears highly probable that both woodpeckers were stressed mainly by excessive human depredations, and that the primary negative effect of timbering on both may have been the increases in shooting that generally accompany the opening up of forested areas by logging activities. The decreases in food supplies produced by timbering may well have been of much less importance. The depredations explanation that Tanner offered for the final demise of the imperial woodpecker in Durango appears to apply equally well to the progressive overall declines of both species, and that the ivory-billed woodpecker in particular might instead have been stressed mainly by habitat destruction is a hypothesis that has special difficulty with the long persistence of the Cuban race of the species in habitat devastated by lumbering activities.

Both habitat degradation and human depredations characterized the period of decline of both woodpecker species, but it has never been well established just how dependent either species may have been on pristine forests. The fact that some of the last populations of these species were associated with such forests may be more a result of relatively infrequent depredations in these forests than a result of any considerations of food availability. Had there been regions of partially degraded forests that were kept completely free of depredations, we would not be surprised to find that such regions continued to be occupied by these species indefinitely, although at population densities somewhat reduced from pristine densities. Thus, the degradation of virtually all virgin forests in the ranges of these species should not in itself be assumed to have precluded the continuing existence of these species. Unfortunately, we know of no forests free of hunting activities within the species' ranges in historical times, and the chance may now have passed to directly test the capacities of either imperials or ivory-bills to endure in degraded forests comprehensively protected from depredations.

Most of the historical strongholds of the ivory-bill we have visited in recent years have long been regions of heavy hunting activity. For example, in a several-day visit to the Wadmacaun Island region of South Carolina's Santee River in the fall of 2003, we were never out of earshot of the detonating weapons of pig and deer hunters, had repeated encounters with hunters and their dogs, and could find few discarded beer cans and other human artifacts that were not riddled with bullet holes. Hunting was also a frequent activity in this same region when Allen and Sprunt (1936: 14) were documenting remnant populations of ivory-bills and Carolina parakeets still in existence:

> The need for an efficient warden service is illustrated by the fact that natives of the region hunt and trap in the unposted Hackney Humes property throughout the year, and while observing Paroquets on the flight line over Boone's Bluff, we could usually hear shots up or down the river within a half mile to a mile of our observation post. The Cooper family appears to do most of the hunting on the Hackney-Humes land and evidently does little else. The most consistent nimrods are Sidney, Daniel, and Glenny Cooper and John Holmes. Occasionally, one of the numerous Lambert family hunts on Hackney-Humes land and a party of hunters that

frequently shoots on the eastern end of Wadmacaun Island on the property of the Brooklyn Cooperage Company may move into the Hackney-Humes portion of the island, or elsewhere up river.

In other words, the very heart of the Paroquet and ivory-bill range is an open shooting ground traversed almost daily throughout the year by the most undesirable type of gunners.

Evidently, at least this part of the Santee region has been risky for ivory-bills for many decades. From the intensity of shooting activities observed during our visit, it seems unlikely that any truly vulnerable species of wildlife could endure in such an area over the long haul, regardless of the quality of forests in the area.

Likewise, in a several-day visit to the Choctawhatchee River bottom-lands of Florida in early 2008—the location of recent unconfirmed reports of ivory-bills discussed by Hill (2007)—we were never out of earshot of gunfire, and repeatedly encountered hunters seeking pigs, deer, and squirrels. None of those we talked to—some of whom had been hunting the region all their lives and apparently knew wildlife well—reported seeing ivory-bills or considered the recent reports of ivory-bills to be valid, although a few visiting bird-watchers we encountered believed they had heard the species. We failed to detect ivory-bills in any location but found spent shells and hunting camps pretty much everywhere.

Similarly, we found evidence for widespread hunting of the White River region of eastern Arkansas when we visited parts of this region in late 2005, and persistence of ivory-bills in this region has not been confirmed despite intensive follow-up by Cornell University personnel of recent sighting reports. Gary Graves of the U.S. National Museum, who has been conducting intensive studies of Swainson's warblers (*Limnothlypis swainsonii*) in this region for a number of years, has likewise never encountered ivory-bills. As Gary put matters in a recent e-mail:

> Thanks for the detailed report of your Choctawhatchee trip. I haven't worked that river but I have a lot of experience with the Escambia, Chipola, Apalachicola, Wakulla, Wacissa, etc. from my years in Tallahassee. The hunting situation is the same throughout the south, including the White River drainage. There is not an acre in the entire White River drainage that isn't trodden by a hunter

or fisherman during the course of a year. City slickers simply can't comprehend the degree to which rural southern people are still connected to the land (and still exploit the hell out of wildlife . . . not that all usage is exploitive). The average soybean farmer in Arkansas spends more time in the woods than 99% of Sierra Club members.

Habitat conditions in these areas (and in many other former haunts of the ivory-bill) still appear to be quite favorable for woodpeckers today, with many large trees standing and many snags and dead limbs offering potential food resources, although all these areas have been subjected to selective logging in the past. Yes, none of these areas is virgin, but that any might lack adequate food supplies to sustain populations of ivory-bills is by no means clear from their structural and biotic characteristics. The present abundance of species such as pileated woodpeckers in many of these areas suggests that ivory-bills might also find them quite congenial from a food standpoint, but the barrage of gunfire characterizing these areas may simply have precluded the persistence of species as highly vulnerable as the ivory-bill. The situation appears to have been entirely similar in the range of the imperial woodpecker, as was well recognized by Plimpton (1977) in his perceptive essay.

To attribute the demise of the ivory-billed and imperial woodpeckers primarily to something so mundane as shooting and other depredations is not nearly as attractive aesthetically as to emphasize the potential dependency of these species on disappearing virgin forests. The image of these species as creatures practically synonymous with towering stands of mature forest carries tremendous emotional appeal. But aesthetics aside, it is important to arrive at a maximally accurate assessment of the causes of decline of these species, because differing causes of decline potentially lead to very different conservation strategies. Although one could well argue for both woodpecker species that we may now be past the point where any conservation actions might be effective, we suggest, nevertheless, that there still is merit in considering such matters in the unlikely event any remnant populations are truly confirmed in the future.

Conservation Considerations

If indeed the primary problem for both the imperial woodpecker and the ivory-bill was unsustainable human depredations, conservation efforts for these species should have been aimed primarily at preventing depredations. For neither species, however, were major conservation investments of any sort ever made historically, and by the time interest in these species rose to levels that might have allowed comprehensive conservation efforts, neither species could be found reliably in the wild.

To his enduring credit, James Tanner (1942, 1964) did not ignore the depredations issue, and in fact he recommended *both* habitat conservation *and* prevention of depredations in his conservation appeals for both species. Nevertheless, the major thrust of Tanner's ivory-bill monograph was that decline of the species was due mainly to habitat considerations, while depredations were portrayed mainly as a potential threat to the last few birds. Perhaps it is not too surprising that conservation discussions for both species ever since have been focused primarily on saving and restoring old-growth and mature forests and not on preventing depredations, despite Tanner's special emphasis on depredations with imperials. In some accounts, problems with depredations are not even mentioned as something needing attention. Indeed, the importance of countering depredation threats has nearly vanished from modern ivory-bill discussions without anyone presenting a persuasive case as to why it might be safe to ignore this issue.

Perhaps in part the general lack of priority given to depredation threats in recent discussions and documents stems from the practical difficulties in detecting and controlling depredations, and to a general distaste for dealing with enforcement issues among conservationists. It may also be a reflection of fears that imposing restrictions on shooting activities could antagonize hunters and potentially produce a backlash directed specifically against these species, although this concern has seldom, if ever, been verbalized. Even more important may be a recognition in resource agencies that hunters represent their most powerful allies and constituents in the public arena, and a desire not to propose any potentially controversial measures that might disturb the support hunters have shown for the agencies and their efforts at wildlife management.

Historical conservation recommendations for ivory-bill habitats were generated for the Singer Tract of Louisiana (Tanner 1942), the Santee River of South Carolina (Allen and Sprunt 1936), the Chipola River of Florida (Eastman 1958), and the region south of Moa in eastern Cuba (Lamb 1957; Short and Horne 1990), but none of the regions in question was extensive, and the amount of real habitat protection achieved ranged from zero to modest. Further, protection was often temporary or implemented only after substantial habitat degradation had already occurred. To be sure, the habitat protection measures developed in these proposals were also coupled with measures to protect these populations from depredations, but there is no evidence that truly comprehensive control of depredations was ever achieved in any of these regions. In any event, ivory-bills disappeared from all these areas.

Similarly, in the case of the imperial woodpecker, Lammertink et al. (1996) focused on efforts to prevent lumbering of some of the last remnant patches of pristine pine forest in the Sierra Madre Occidental. However, the habitat recommendations of Lammertink et al. were not so much recommendations on behalf of the imperial as recommendations aimed at the conservation of other species and old-growth forest in general, as these authors expressed little optimism about the continued existence of imperials in the areas in question. Uranga-Thomas and Venegas-Holguin (1995) likewise recommended creation of reserves of favorable habitat, not so much for imperials as for other species still in existence. Only Tanner (1964) focused mainly on the necessity of stopping depredations in his conservation recommendations for imperials, although he also recommended creation of habitat preserves.

Thus, habitat conservation efforts on behalf of ivory-bills and imperials have been only modest in scale and have generally come too late to offer much, if any, benefit to remnant populations. And if we are correct in concluding that human depredations were the primary cause of decline of both species, conservation efforts would likely have failed even if major tracts of virgin forest had been preserved intact, unless truly effective control of human depredations had been achieved simultaneously. Much as habitat conservation is an important general conservation need, and much as it would almost surely have been beneficial for both species, it alone may never have had the potential to ensure survival of either.

These remarks should not be interpreted to indicate opposition to habitat preservation efforts, but should be considered a plea that habitat conservation efforts be placed in proper perspective. It is important to recognize that habitat conservation is not always the primary imperative in saving endangered species. For example, substantial habitat conservation efforts have not in themselves produced recovery in the California condor or the masked bobwhite (*Colinus virginianus ridgwayi*), and habitat preservation has not been a sufficient approach for saving various disease-threatened native birds of Hawaii (see Brown 1985a; Snyder and Snyder 2000, 2005; Warner 1968; van Riper and Scott 2001; van Riper et al. 1986; van Riper, van Riper, and Hansen 2002). Habitat issues have also been of subsidiary importance in the endangerment and recovery of other threatened charismatic birds, for example, many species threatened by pesticide contaminants during the organochlorine era after World War II (see Newton 1979).

Perhaps in seeking parallel cases to the ivory-bill and imperial woodpeckers, we should look toward the whooping crane (*Grus americana*) and the trumpeter swan (*Cygnus buccinator*), two North American species highly vulnerable to the gun that were driven to very low numbers mainly by intense shooting pressures during the late nineteenth and early twentieth centuries (see R. P. Allen 1952; Banko 1960). Reductions in shooting pressures for these two species, achieved in part by the creation of no-hunting preserves, came barely in time to allow recovery, but not all of the shooting-stressed species of this period were so fortunate (e.g., Eskimo curlews, *Numenius borealis*). It is worth noting that most of the extinctions and near extinctions of avian species in North America in the nineteenth and early twentieth centuries involved species that were vulnerable to shooting and other depredations because they were reasonably large and were regarded as game or were valuable for their feathers or other body parts. Besides whooping cranes, trumpeter swans, and Eskimo curlews, other well-known examples include the great auk (*Pinguinus impennis*), the Labrador duck (*Camptorhynchus labradorius*), and the passenger pigeon (*Ectopistes migratorius*). The slaughter of wildlife that took place during this era traced in no small measure to the development of much improved firearms technology and was so devastating in magnitude that many species of medium to large vertebrates were eliminated from large portions of their ranges (see discussion in J. A. Allen 1876 and Steinhart 1999).

The imperial and ivory-billed woodpeckers provide two more examples of species stressed historically by shooting pressures, and it may now be too late to preserve either one, although this is not an absolute certainty. The recent reported rediscoveries of the ivory-bill in Arkansas (Fitzpatrick et al. 2005) and Florida (Hill et al. 2006) have raised hopes that remnant populations may still exist. They have also provided a major stimulus for the reevaluation of potential causes of the species' declines.

The development of truly effective recovery actions for remnant populations may hinge crucially on the quality of such analyses. Yes, presumably all conservationists would favor both the preservation of habitat and the prevention of depredations for both species, at least as a generality. But this consensus does not take us very far in resolving how priorities and resources might best be allocated in recovery efforts.

In very recent years, as in the more distant past, far more attention has been given to habitat protection for the ivory-bill than to preventing depredations. In Arkansas, for example, recent ivory-bill conservation efforts have been focused mainly on a substantial habitat-acquisition effort by the U.S. Fish and Wildlife Service and The Nature Conservancy. Little has been publicized about preventing depredations, except a section of the federal hunting and fishing regulations for the region that discusses and illustrates field marks of the ivory-bill to enhance the reporting of sightings and to reduce chances of ignorant shootings (USFWS 2005).

In fact, ivory-bill conservation in Arkansas has been promoted as largely compatible with, and even beneficial for, traditional hunting activities (see Wiedensaul 2005: 31). Shooting has not been identified in public documents as an important contributing, let alone major, cause of the species' endangerment, and instead hunters have been credited as being "largely responsible for saving the IBW" through habitat purchases made possible by Duck Stamp funding (USFWS 2005). Even the draft recovery plan for the ivory-billed woodpecker (USFWS 2006) offers no comprehensive discussion of needs to control depredations in current and future conservation efforts and is overwhelmingly slanted toward habitat preservation and enhancement goals.

Nevertheless, even though James Tanner too believed habitat loss was the major cause of the species' decline, he was sufficiently concerned about human depredations that in his conservation recommendations (Tanner 1942: 100) he urged that the ivory-bill be accorded "complete protection from man by the barring of all hunters and collectors from areas inhabited by the woodpecker." For a species as endangered and as vulnerable to depredations as the ivory-bill, Tanner's recommendations do not seem unreasonable or outdated. Wanton and mistaken shootings of protected species continue to occur with some frequency today, and it is not clear that an adequate level of safety from depredations can be achieved in the absence of well-enforced closure of crucial ivory-bill areas to shooting.

Presumably the areas needing such protection are not just specific locations where ivory-bills are discovered initially, but also substantial adjacent regions to permit and promote expansion of remnant populations. Access and hunting closures for the ivory-bill in Arkansas have been limited so far to a temporary closure, now long-since terminated, of a 5,000-acre stretch of Bayou de View in the Cache River National Wildlife Refuge, where the first recent ivory-bill sightings were reported—by no means the only location for recent audio and visual reports of the species in the region (although, to be sure, all of these reports remain controversial). The federal government is presently in the somewhat schizophrenic position of continuing to assert the validity of recent rediscovery of the species in Arkansas and pouring money into habitat and other conservation measures for the species, including development of a recovery plan, but at the same time not providing any continuing exclusion of hunters or anyone else from areas where the birds have been reported.

Focusing on the values of preventing habitat loss and encouraging the public to believe that successful conservation of ivory-bills can be achieved without significant sacrifice of hunting privileges on lands where ivory-bills occur may be politically attractive because these policies minimize immediate opposition to conservation efforts. But efforts limited to such policies may well be too timid to be effective in conserving the species. Especially in regions where hunters have had a major positive role in preserving bottomland forests from destruction, and seek, with considerable justification, to ensure hunting rights into the future, the closure of lands to protect the ivory-bill can be expected to be controversial. Yet for a reasonable chance of success with ivory-bill or imperial woodpecker recovery, it appears essential that the needs of remnant populations for safety from shooting be recognized and accommodated in a truly effective manner.

Some observers (e.g., Hill 2007) picture contemporary ivory-bills (if they truly exist) as being so extremely wary of humanity that they need no extra protection from shooting, but it is difficult to believe that any woodpecker species, no matter how wary, might be capable of consistently avoiding situations of vulnerability to shooters. Ivory-bills and imperials, by their very nature, need to move substantial distances through their environments in search of food, and their feeding activities are intrinsically noisy. Even if the potential wariness of contemporary individuals might make them difficult to stalk, there presumably will still be occasions when they blunder into close proximity to hunters that they do not detect in time to avoid (for a vivid description of such an encounter, see Hasbrouck 1891: 181). While we agree that the majority of U.S. hunters today would not be likely to shoot ivory-bills, except by mistake, the recent and continuing losses to shooting of fully protected and easily identified species such as the California condor and the whooping crane give evidence that no species of appreciable size is secure from ignorant or malicious depredations in regions where shooting activities occur. Failing to exclude shooters from use areas of ivory-bills and imperials does not appear to be a safe or conservative conservation strategy.

We submit that until ivory-bill and imperial populations are truly out of extreme endangerment, no losses to shooting and other depredations should be tolerated in recovery efforts, and this does indeed mean exclusion of shooting activities from confirmed use areas by whatever means may be feasible. The reserves at Aransas in Texas and Red Rock Lakes in Montana that appear to have been crucial in allowing recovery of the whooping crane and the trumpeter swan, respectively, were established specifically to conserve these species by protecting them from shooting, rather than to promote traditional hunting activities. It is only prudent to assume that such protection would be essential for any ivory-bill or imperial population unambiguously rediscovered today.

Rediscovery and Recovery of Remnant Populations

But what indeed are the chances of rediscovering remnant ivory-bill or imperial populations that might serve as a basis for recovery of these species? None of the recent reports of these species has yet been followed by confirmation of the birds' existence through clearly diagnostic photographs or video, repeated detailed sightings at roost or nest holes by qualified observers, or other persuasive evidence that might lead to universal acceptance of the reports. Like the rest of the world, we still hope that such confirmation may yet be achieved somewhere and allow the development of focused and successful recovery efforts. But especially in the case of the ivory-bill in the United States, we nonetheless believe that the chances for confirmation of remnant populations appear to be slim and dwindling with time in view of the inconclusive results of the major confirmation efforts that have already been made.

In part, the efforts to locate remnant populations have proceeded on assumptions that have arguably been too narrow to maximize the chances of success. In recent times, searches for these species have been limited almost entirely to regions with relatively mature forests (see Jackson 2004; Gallagher 2005; Lammertink et al. 1996), while other areas lacking such impressive forests have been neglected on the assumption that the species could not exist in such areas. But if the primary stress for these species really has been human depredations, not habitat degradation, success may be increased by expanding efforts to include areas that have been relatively free of shooting activities for long periods, if any can be found, even if they are only moderately forested areas. Searches limited to areas with near-pristine timber resources could miss some remnant populations.

Thus, the chances of finding ivory-bills today may be higher in Cuba, the country where the last well-documented population of ivory-bills resided, than in the United States. To be sure, massive loss and degradation of forests has occurred in Cuba but, of major significance, governmental policies have greatly reduced the use of firearms island-wide, and a few forested areas have been maintained off-limits to human access for nearly a half century. A number of promising regions of Cuba have not yet been subjected to intensive searching despite the admirable efforts of Lammertink and Estrada (1995) and others, and it is well to remember that Cuba is a very large island (more than 700 miles in length), with a former ivory-bill range extending from one end to the other.

Let us suppose for the moment that the ivory-bill might be rediscovered in small, but potentially recoverable, numbers somewhere in Cuba. The question then becomes what sort of actions might be taken to maximize the chances of true recovery. Given Cuba's system of government and already established policies greatly limiting firearms use, we would rate the potential for recovering the species as relatively good if the government were to make the prevention of depredations a priority. However, we know from Lamb's (1957) study that shooting is not the only depredations threat to the species on this island, and it is reasonable to assume that major education and enforcement efforts would have to be made to prevent *all* forms of depredations in regions still occupied by the species and identified for expansion of the species. We would also recommend, to be sure, that substantial efforts be made to preserve and enhance forested habitats wherever remnant populations might be found, and that a major research program be initiated to reveal any and all other factors that might be affecting the viability of these populations.

Rediscovery of the species in Cuba could also lead to pressures from some U.S. interests to translocate ivory-bills from Cuba to the United States, assuming that by that time confirmation of any U.S. populations remains lacking. But unless U.S. officials come to recognize the threats posed by depredations on their own turf and take appropriate steps to truly protect the species from such threats, we believe such translocations might well fail to result in viable U.S. populations and could at the same time diminish the chances for species recovery in Cuba. As already discussed, there are few signs of enthusiasm for controls on depredation threats as a component of ivory-bill conservation in the United States, despite Tanner's clear recommendations on this subject.

In any event, we strongly doubt that most Cuban conservationists would favor any sort of international translocations of Cuban ivory-bills under present circumstances, and indeed if the suggestion of Fleischer et al. (2006) might be adopted—that the Cuban ivory-bill should be considered a separate species from the mainland ivory-bill—moving birds from Cuba to the United States would constitute introduction of an alien species, not reintroduction to reestablish an extirpated population of a native species. We are not here expressing an opinion as to whether the Cuban population should be rated a separate species, but perhaps the reader can sense our basic fears regarding the risks of translocation efforts, at least during initial stages of attempting to recover a Cuban population. Indeed, from the standpoint of depredations threats, a stronger case could probably be made for moving ivory-bills rediscovered in the United States to Cuba than the reverse, although there are significant risks with movements in either direction.

Recovery of indigenous ivory-bill populations in the United States strikes us as potentially more difficult than recovery of Cuban populations, despite the existence of some impressive bottomland forests in the United States that have regenerated well since the era of heavy timbering in the early twentieth century. In the event that a remnant population might truly be confirmed in the United States, the primary difficulty in achieving its resuscitation may well lie in achieving adequate control of depredations when (1) most interested parties are still convinced that the only problem needing correction for the ivory-bill is availability of mature forests, (2) powerful private and public organizations favor making maximum areas of mature forest available for hunting activities, and (3) effectively enforcing no-hunting restrictions for forested areas can pose substantial practical difficulties. In most regions, overcoming these difficulties will presumably entail major education efforts, major political difficulties in creating no-hunting reserves, and major continuing investments in enforcement activities. Perhaps the most difficult, yet most essential, task is achieving a consensus that ivory-bills need to be given thorough protection against the threats of depredations.

The challenges inherent in recovering a remnant imperial woodpecker population, like those entailed with the recovery of a U.S. ivory-bill population, are daunting. The range of the imperial in the Sierra Madre Occidental is largely wide open to unregulated hunting, and law enforcement of any sort in this region faces tremendous obstacles, as large regions are under illegal drug cultivation and are dangerous to enter for any reason, as we have seen first-hand in studies of the thick-billed parrot (*Rhynchopsitta pachyrhyncha*). Resident human populations have had a long history of killing imperial woodpeckers for food and medicinal purposes, and even though there have been potentially valid reports of this species as recently as the 1990s (see Lammertink et al. 1996), the practical difficulties in ensuring safety of any remnant population from depredations would be formidable.

The difficulties faced are clear from the fact that hunting regulations have not made most game species abundant in the Sierra Madre Occidental. Game wardens are few, and the chances of game-law offenders being caught are low. And while it is true that parts of the Sierra Madre look much the same as they did in Nelson's, Sheldon's and W. W. Brown's day, the larger wildlife species found by those visitors are now much diminished in this great mountain fastness. White-tailed deer (*Odocoileus virginianus couesi*), although widely distributed, are now few in number almost everywhere but in hunting reserves. And, despite vague, unsubstantiated reports to the contrary, there is no evidence that grizzlies (*Ursus horribilis*) now exist anywhere in Mexico, the last of their kind being killed in the Sierra del Nido in Chihuahua in the 1950s and early 1960s. Several expeditions in search of *oso grande* since then have been unable to produce a hair, a plaster cast of a track, a recognizable photograph, or any other verification of a living grizzly. Even the more adaptable black bear (*Ursus americanus*) persists only in a few outlying ranges, where it is afforded a modicum of legal and geographic protection. The Mexican wolf, or *lobo*, (*Canis lupus baileyi*) is also gone, its presence reduced to a few captive animals maintained at La Michilía Biosphere Reserve in the state of Durango. Alas, the imperial woodpecker may also be extinct. As yet, few inviolate wildlife sanctuaries to protect such species exist in the Sierra Madre Occidental, although interest and success in creating such reserves is on the increase in very recent years, due in part to the recognition of the very high biodiversity values of the region (see DeBano et al. 1995). Despite the loss of some of its most charismatic megavertebrates, this region still maintains a marvelous variety of species that are not considered game or threats to domestic animals and crops.

Thus, even if remnant populations of ivory-bills or imperials might be found, achieving recovery of these populations in the wild may well prove difficult in practical terms—largely for the same basic reasons that these species became endangered in the first place. Nevertheless, we believe that the greatest chances of success in reviving these species would lie in facing limiting factors in the wild squarely and carefully prioritizing efforts to counter the most significant problems effectively. We hold little hope that the alternative approach of captive breeding might offer significant benefits. When the correction of limiting factors in the wild proves difficult, those involved in recovery programs often feel compelled to recommend captive breeding, with the justification that captive populations will buy time for the more challenging task of correcting basic problems in the wild. But captive breeding has substantial intrinsic limitations, and can often serve more as an excuse not to deal with fundamental problems in the wild than as a technique aiding the solution of these problems. As discussed by Snyder et al. (1996), captive breeding is simply not promising as a long-term conservation technique and is usually a very expensive technique if implemented comprehensively. It should be invoked only when no other options exist for preserving species in the short term.

Husbandry techniques are not presently well developed for captive populations of any large woodpeckers and, even if they were, challenges in achieving adequate disease control and preventing genetic and behavioral deterioration in captivity, not to mention the frequent difficulties encountered in reintroducing captive stocks to the wild, make the captive approach problematic. Current complications in trying to produce normally behaving wild populations of California condors from captive stocks give warning of the height of the hurdles that can be posed by pursuit of such techniques (see Mee and Hall 2007). For higher vertebrates, problems can be especially severe when all individuals of a species wind up in captivity, and captives reintroduced to the wild have to reinvent adaptive wild behaviors from scratch with no opportunities to learn from wild-experienced individuals.

Overall, the chances that either the ivory-bill or the imperial woodpecker can still be recovered must be considered remote at best. As we write this overview, there are no uncontested indications that any populations of these species exist at all. So long as this continues to be true, it is legitimate to ask whether spending major resources, at least public conservation resources, on efforts to find and recover these species is warranted. These are indeed tremendously charismatic birds, and surely achieving successful conservation of these species would aid the conservation of many other species sharing their ranges. But most programs today for endangered species that still surely exist are desperately starved for resources. Diverting major sums that could be spent on their behalf to searches for creatures that may no longer exist appears difficult to justify. In the United States such actions appear to be inconsistent with basic charges of the federal Endangered Species Act (U.S. Congress 1973), which directs the interior secretary to "give priority to those endangered species or threatened species, without regard to taxonomic classification, that are most likely to benefit from such plans" (sec. 4.f.1.).

So while we support continued efforts to find "lost" species, such as ivory-bills, imperials, and Bachman's warblers (*Vermivora bachmanii*), and can think of little that would be more uplifting than success in this regard, we support such efforts with the caveat that they should not come at the expense of jeopardizing other less charismatic threatened species. Endangered species programs do indeed compete for limited conservation resources, and at least in the United States, allocation of substantial public sums to searches for extinct species or likely extinct species stretches the intent of the Endangered Species Act in potentially dangerous directions. Recent history has shown that many people are willing to donate their private resources and time to searching for ivory-bills and imperials. We believe that privately funded efforts should be the emphasis until remnant populations are truly confirmed. In Cuba, however, the involvement of governmental personnel in searches may be essential, especially because strictly private access to some promising areas would probably be impossible to achieve.

Ways to Improve Conservation Efforts

In reviewing the history of decline toward extinction of any species, we would be negligent not to discuss fundamental problems that have led to unnecessary mistakes and missed opportunities. The histories of the ivory-billed and imperial woodpeckers provide many examples of events and strategies that if they had played out a bit differently might not have led to the probable loss of the species. In this final section we review a number of such issues that, even though they are probably "water over the dam" for ivory-bills and imperials, have potential importance for improving future conservation efforts with other endangered species.

First and foremost, the main motivation for producing this book has been to examine the implications of an alternative hypothesis for the decline of the ivory-billed and imperial woodpeckers that we believe has long been undervalued. Whatever hypotheses one might favor for the causes of decline of endangered species, the main effort should be not to just find support for these hypotheses but to examine alternative hypotheses as well and to obtain crucial data that can help reveal which hypotheses are most likely correct. It is only by careful and respectful elimination of alternative explanations that one is likely to advance toward the truth. This is nothing more than the basic scientific method, although it is remarkable how often scientists, sadly including ourselves, deviate from these procedures and either ignore relevant conflicting data or spend enormous energies trying to rationalize data that are just not supportive of favored preconceptions.

As a case in point with the ivory-bill, we find it instructive to reflect on how many modern publications have either ignored or gone through contortions to dismiss the many early records of the abundance of this species and have continued to advocate a belief that the species was always a rare food specialist dependent on huge areas of pristine forest. It is difficult to find any support for this belief in early writings, other than the typical association of the species with mature forests. This association, however, is hardly sufficient to prove feeding specialization, and if, instead of dominating conservation thought, the feeding-specialization hypothesis had been recognized at the outset as only a weakly substantiated possibility, depredations might enjoy much wider recognition as likely the major problem for this species. Indeed, if effective actions to preclude depredations had been taken in a few critical areas, we believe there is a reasonable chance that vigorous populations of this species might still exist today, despite at least partial timbering of nearly all of our original eastern forests.

Another basic issue that is well illustrated by the history of research efforts with the ivory-bill is the need to closely examine the extent of variability in a population of any organism before generalizing about what may be true of the organism as an entire population or species. Sample sizes limited to data on single pairs are a dangerous basis for sweeping generalizations, as was well recognized by Tanner in the introduction to his monograph. Yet certain long-accepted conclusions about the species, for example the belief in bark-stripping foraging preferences, are not immune to this very criticism. Tanner was able to make detailed observations of only a single pair over the several years of his studies, but this pair may not have been typical of the species in foraging characteristics due to peculiar constraints of timber availability in its range. If Tanner instead had been able to emphasize comparisons among pairs facing a variety of timber-availability situations, we could have much more confidence about his conclusions regarding foraging characteristics of the species in general.

With the imperial woodpecker, it is difficult to understand why no professional ornithologists or conservationists made any concerted efforts to locate and study the species in the early twentieth century, when it appears there were still appreciable populations in existence. Tanner got to Durango apparently just a bit too late to find the species in the early 1960s, but it evidently would have been possible to have conducted very informative studies on the species in the 1940s and 1950s. It is not clear that anyone in particular should be blamed for the general neglect of studies on the imperial, but as matters developed, this species, the largest and most magnificent woodpecker in the world, never received any truly comprehensive research. The great bulk of the very limited information on its biology comes from a single brief account by Nelson in the 1890s. We will probably never really know what chances may have existed for conserving this species.

Also very regrettable is the fact that studies of the rediscovered ivory-bill population in Cuba were put on hold with the socialist revolution that reached its culmination in 1959. There were still at least a half dozen pairs in existence in this population in 1956, and if these pairs had been given concerted attention, enough might have been learned and accomplished to have headed off extirpation of the population. As things turned out, it was not until the mid-1980s that ornithologists were again able to mount any efforts for this population, and by then it was evidently too late. Martjan Lammertink (1995: 46) remarked, "Perhaps *C. principalis* holds the dubious honour of being the one species that was exterminated by the Cold War." But the problem of lapsed conservation efforts for the Cuban ivory-bills may have had multiple causes beyond strained relations between the United States and Cuba.

Another population for which we have strong regrets was the ivory-bill population along the Santee River of South Carolina that evidently persisted into the late 1930s (see Allen and Sprunt 1936; Snyder 2004; plate 2). Shortly after discovery of this population in 1935, plans were underway to make a sanctuary out of the lands in question and otherwise protect the population, together with a population of Carolina parakeets reported for the same location. Sadly, these plans were aborted largely because of the extreme skepticism of the influential ornithologist Ludlow Griscom, who unfortunately did not see either ivory-bills or Carolina parakeets on his one trip to the region in 1937 and wrote a highly dismissive report regarding values of the region (although other capable ornithologists had reported both species there at close range and the balance of evidence appears to support their claims). As two highly endangered and charismatic species were involved in this affair, it is perhaps doubly tragic that conservation efforts simply collapsed there after Griscom's visit.

The history of events along the Santee provides a striking example of the potential penalties that can be entailed in rejecting sight records of highly endangered species when they may really be true. But on the other side of the coin are the penalties that can result from accepting such reports when they are not authentic. When huge amounts of money become invested on the basis of apparently credible reports that turn out not to be well supported, such investments are not only of no value to the species in question, but can sometimes jeopardize other endangered species that might otherwise have received the resources invested (see Jackson 2006). Such errors can also undermine the general credibility of conservationists and conservation efforts with the public. The stakes are high, with errors in either direction having major consequences. Reputations often stand or fall on such matters in an astonishingly vicious way.

Clearly before definitive judgments are made about rediscovery of species that have been long considered extinct, there is a need for very careful evaluations of apparently credible sightings (see McKelvey, Aubry, and Schwartz 2008), and such evaluations should deliberately involve people holding a wide diversity of viewpoints—skeptics as well as advocates. But even then we should not be surprised to see errors in judgment prevail in some instances.

Bona fide rediscoveries of species thought potentially extinct do occur on occasion, for example, that of the masked bobwhite (Gallizioli, Levy, and Levy 1967), and some have led to successful recovery efforts. Outstanding examples of programs with rediscovered species that appear to be heading toward recovery include those involving the kakapo (*Strigops habroptilus*) in New Zealand, the cahow (*Pterodroma cahow*) in Bermuda, and the black-footed ferret (*Mustela nigripes*) in the United States, difficult as success has been to achieve. No one would be well advised to completely rule out something similar occurring with ivory-bills or imperials even today, despite our general pessimism over such prospects. And if remnant populations of these species are indeed truly confirmed someday, we hope that a consideration of the issues discussed in this book might aid in designing effective strategies for recovery. If no such populations still exist, however, we hope our review may at least help provide a better understanding of why they have disappeared.

Concluding Remarks

The imperial and ivory-billed woodpeckers were two of the most magnificent flying creatures inhabiting our primeval forests. The forests without them today, and without the Carolina parakeets, the passenger pigeons, and the Bachman's warblers that all still existed only a century ago, no longer look or sound the same. Yet as we explore remote woodlands today, it is impossible not to hope or imagine that all these species might still exist somewhere, perhaps unnoticed in some corner that no one has thought to search. We cannot logically exclude the possibility that one or more of these species might miraculously reappear, but at the same time we are also aware that many of these species were actually quite noisy and conspicuous, and there are now few, if any, areas of truly untrammeled wilderness where they might safely hide from view. Proponents of their continued existence sometimes find themselves proclaiming that these species have become so incredibly wary and silent that they can never be properly observed by human eyes, let alone photographed. But alas, a more likely explanation for the absence of persuasively confirmed reports is that all these species are now gone forever.

We mourn the probable loss of these birds, but it is no secret that they may soon be followed into oblivion by many other creatures. The full dimensions of the extinction crisis that is widely predicted for the near future are yet to be seen and may lead to regrets far more powerful than the primarily aesthetic sorrows we experience now for a few recently departed species. A planet missing many of the species still in existence today may well prove a much less hospitable place for our own existence in many unsuspected, yet irreversible, ways.

Species conservation is often perceived as a matter of aesthetics and ethics, but it is much more than that. Surely, we all have a practical stake in attempting to prevent the demise of as many of our fellow species as can be achieved, if only to preserve the maximum number of options for the future in an increasingly unstable world, where interactions with other species are still fundamental to our existence but are constantly changing in ways that are often impossible to predict. Highly charismatic species such as the imperial and ivory-billed woodpeckers fill an extremely important role in symbolizing and epitomizing natural ecosystems and in developing an acute awareness of the importance of conservation for us all. These values have not been a matter of debate in the countless articles and other presentations that have appeared recently on these species in our diverse media, and they have been recognized, either implicitly or explicitly, in numerous historical writings.

The sad part is that our own species has not succeeded in conserving these magnificent creatures, and very likely the chances of ever doing so have now been lost. Yet there is no reason to believe that preservation of these species was beyond possibility or practicality while they still existed. Perhaps we all share some of the blame for their loss, and we all surely share the consequences. But at least let us hope that our species can do much better in rescuing other highly valued species descending into the spiral of endangerment in the future.

MISDIAGNOSED
CAUSES OF DECLINE

Management is conserving particular plants or animals by keeping the land favorable.

—ALDO LEOPOLD, *Biotic land-use*, ca. 1942

Education, I fear is learning to see one thing by going blind in another.

—ALDO LEOPOLD, *A Sand County almanac*, 1949

Habitat preservation has long been recognized by ecologists as a primary necessity in species conservation efforts. We ourselves have endorsed this principle on many occasions, as all species, after all, must have adequate amounts of appropriate habitat to survive. But beyond this basic truism, the belief that "habitat is everything" has become a mantra of modern wildlife management. Indeed, such statements as "if you look after the habitat, you look after the species" and "most all extinctions are due to habitat destruction" and "no species ever vanished due to regulated hunting" have become commonplace assessments in the day-to-day world of wildlife agencies.

Nevertheless, many species populations have proven surprisingly tolerant of habitat change, while others have shown major fluctuations in spite of relative stability of their habitats. If for no other reason than so many species have greatly declined or disappeared while significant portions of their habitats have remained intact, our profession's mantra is in need of some reexamination.

Examples of disappearances that have probably been largely independent of habitat loss include a broad range of extinctions ranging from southwestern grizzlies (*Ursus arctos horribilis*) and the eastern panther (*Puma concolor couguar*) through to the great auk (*Pinguinus impennis*), Carolina parakeet (*Conuropsis carolinensis*), and Labrador duck (*Camptorhynchus labradorius*). Adding to the list such poorly understood extirpations and endangerments as Bachman's warbler (*Vermivora bachmanii*), Attwater's prairie chicken (*Tympanchus cupido attwateri*), and masked bobwhite (*Colinus virginianus ridgwayi*) gives some idea of the conundrums involved. That at least some of these species continued to decline and disappear after habitats had been acquired and preserved specifically for their benefit strongly suggests that more than habitat loss has probably been at work.

The principal causes of the decline of endangered species are often quite difficult to determine. But if effective recovery measures are to be designed and implemented, these causes need to be well understood so that limited conservation resources are not aimed in the wrong direction. Habitat protection is usually a helpful enterprise in recovery programs, but it is often not the most pressing priority, and alone it may often be insufficient to rescue species from the brink of extinction. Yes, it does provide benefits for whole ecosystems, rather than just for single species, but when the preservation of valued single species is of paramount concern, a focus on habitat matters can sometimes steal resources and attention from other more crucial conservation actions, leaving these actions inadequately addressed. Further, where implemented and not truly needed, expensive habitat acquisitions can sometimes usurp resources from conservation efforts for other species in dire need of assistance.

The reasons for losing species are diverse and sometimes complex, sometimes simple. California condors (*Gymnogyps californianus*) declined and nearly perished in substantial part due to various poisons in their carrion food and not primarily because of habitat destruction. Many species of Hawaiian birds succumbed with the establishment of mosquito vectors for bird malaria in the archipelago. Efforts to reestablish woodland caribou (*Rangifer tarandus caribou*) in the United States failed due to a brain disease transmitted by infected populations of white-tailed deer (*Odocoileus virginianus*). A lack of resistance to new (i.e., exotic) diseases may also explain other disappearances or declines, such as those of the black-footed ferret (*Mustela nigripes*) and yellow-billed magpie (*Pica nuttalli*). Nobody really knows what happened to Bachman's warbler. Other species, such as the great auk, the California grizzly (*Ursus arctos californicus*), and the American bison (*Bison bison*) were simply hunted to extinction or near extinction. Human depredations, exotic pathogens, introduced predators, environmental contaminants, and a host of other negative forces often turn out to be the primary culprits when adequate studies are made. In our judgment, habitat loss heads the list of probable adverse factors for relatively few of the avian extinctions already documented for North America, although there are some examples, such as the dusky seaside sparrow (*Ammodramas maritimus nigrescens*).

Perhaps not surprisingly, habitat protection has had only a mixed record of success in preserving endangered species. Yes, habitat reserves, especially when combined with effective protection against human depredations, have indeed been the salvation of some species, witness whooping cranes (*Grus americana*) and trumpeter swans (*Cygnus buccinator*). But biologists have been releasing pen-reared masked bobwhites (*Colinus virginianus ridgwayi*) into apparently good habitat on the Buenos Aires National Wildlife Refuge in Arizona for more than twenty-five years without reestablishing a viable population. Management plans call for doing more of the same. Peregrines (*Falco peregrinus*) and bald eagles (*Haliaeetus leucocephalus*) recovered pretty much with no attention to habitat matters once DDE and Dieldrin residues declined. Red wolves (*Canis niger*) continue to find adequate habitat for existence but continue to crossbreed themselves out of existence with coyotes (*Canis latrans*) and must be artificially maintained. Other species, such as the Colorado grizzlies, while endowed with suitable habitats, are still not locally tolerated by our own species. There's good habitat in the San Juan Mountains, but it won't sustain bears unless managers can find a way to keep local stock-raisers from killing them.

One consequence of species being absent from their preferred habitats is a proliferation of the phenomenon known as cryptozoology—the search in suitable-appearing habitats for potentially extinct animals that should be there. Sometimes, as in the case of the black-footed ferret, the species sought may actually be found. More often, however, as in the case with the eastern panther, the search may continue on without resolution for decades. Proving a negative is an ever-open proposition, subject to an unending flow of debatable sound recordings, blurred images, and other inconclusive evidence. Even seasoned biologists have been known to expend much energy and not a little treasure on false hopes.

Clearly, in attempting to achieve maximal effectiveness and efficiency in rescuing endangered species, we need to deploy available resources wisely. Often this entails a focus on another basic tenet of wildlife management that was early emphasized by Aldo Leopold (1933)—a search for crucial limiting factors. The complexity of interactions of species with adverse forces is far too great to allow a reliance on simplistic habitat protection as a formula panacea for saving threatened forms. The penalties for not conducting high-quality research into limiting factors and for basing decisions instead on armchair speculations are many and range from the frittering away of scarce resources to the declines in morale that inevitably result from pursuing ineffective conservation strategies.

The highest cost of failing to identify primary limiting factors is that many species that might otherwise be saved will probably be lost, especially through the failure to begin effective recovery actions while there still might be time to reverse population declines. Prompt corrective action can be especially important in those cases where the primary limiting factor is humanity's outright persecution of a species, whether for food, sport, trophies, specimens, medicinal purposes, simple curiosity, or reductions in threats to crops and livestock. Had what we believe were the true primary causes for the imperilment of the ivory-billed and imperial woodpeckers been more widely recognized in the 1930s and 1940s, and had an effort been made to change people's behavior toward these birds and establish truly safe sanctuaries for them, one or both of these species might have persisted in viable populations into the twenty-first century. As it is, we are now faced with the potential loss of two of the most incredible birds native to North America.

APPENDIX 1

Letters of Arthur T. Wayne to Frank Chapman in 1905

Mount Pleasant, S.C., Aug. 23, 1905

Mr. Frank M. Chapman

Dear Sir:

The Ivory-bill is *still* an abundant bird in certain localities in N.W. Florida as I well know. I believe I have seen more of these woodpeckers than any man living, and in different portions of N.W. Florida I have seen upwards of 200 of these magnificent birds.

If you will go to the Aucilla River, or better still, the Wacissa, and descend the latter stream to the "Canal Hammock," then go *East* you will get into a great inland swamp which runs to the Econfina River. If you go *West* from the Wacissa (where it empties into the Aucilla) you go in the direction of St. Marks.

There is an enormous inland swamp near the Florida "Volcano" and you will find numbers of Ivory-bills. No one has *ever* been into that "Volcano" region (which lies west of the Wacissa River) collecting specimens except the writer and I got out of it as quickly as I could.

There is a magnificent swampy hammock *off* the Suwannee River *near* Week's Landing, in *Levy* County where there are today numbers of Ivory-bills. Any cracker will accompany you to the place, which is known as "Suwannee Hammock." The Ivory-bill is a bird of the *inland* swamps, and *not* the river swamps, and the centre of abundance of these birds is between the Suwannee River and about 8 or 10 miles *East* of St. Marks— bordering the coast. There is practically an unbroken inland swamp from near the mouth of the Suwannee to St. Marks Light House. If I can be of further assistance to you by giving minute details; people with whom you can stay, guides etc., I will be very glad to do so. The Ivory bill is a *rare* bird on the Florida peninsula as I well know.

Very truly yours,

Arthur T. Wayne

Mount Pleasant, S.C., Oct. 12, 1905

Mr. Frank M. Chapman,

Dear Sir:

After mailing a card to you yesterday about the warbler notes I sent, I have received your letter today. I am very glad you received the letter as I spent more than four hours searching for the earliest and latest dates— ever since 1884!

I did not know that Mr. Helms ever visited the Wacissa, but it is very evident that he did not spend many days in that region, therefore he is not a competent person to judge the rarity or abundance of the Ivory-bill! I spent *many* months in the Aucilla and Wacissa regions as well as *two* seasons on the Suwannee. In regard to "Capt." Jack I do not even *now* know where he killed his "forty" specimens, but I do know that I was instrumental in bringing him to account. Mr. Dutcher can tell you the role I played in the "Jack" episode!

I have often regretted publishing the account of my observations on the birds of the Aucilla and Wacissa rivers, and particularly about the Ivory-bills. Mr. Brewster advised me to publish it provided I did not care to go there again, and Dr. Allen also advised me to include it in my article, but to eliminate the numbers taken and observed. I know that I *left* more than *100* birds in a radius of 20 square miles.

I was very sick while I was in Waukeenah. If any man can stand the *awful stench* of the Wacissa river (in May) he must have a powerful constitution. I purposely prolonged my stay in order to satisfy myself, beyond a doubt, if there was a "Snail Hawk" to be found in that region, and I was not disappointed, as I found the Everglade Kite to be a common bird in May—none breeding, however. The birds simply wander from their breeding grounds (in southern Fla) to feed upon the snails which are to be seen in millions in the Wacissa. It would require years to explore (even a part of) the great inland swamps in Levy, Jefferson, Lafayette and Taylor Counties, Florida.

If Jack has exterminated the Ivory-bills on the Wacissa (and I doubt it as he or no one else can do it) there are many places left in which I know where there are many Ivory-bills. If you will go to Branford and cross the Suwannee, almost any cracker will take you to "Brushy Hammock" and "Pumpkin Swamp" where no one has collected except the writer. The San Pedro Bay runs through two counties and must contain innumerable Ivory-bills today. I could write a volume on the Ivory-bill, and I believe that I have seen and taken more birds of this species than any man. I have been offered large sums of money to go to Florida to get these birds and their eggs, but I have declined an offer up to date. I have the finest specimens in existence today in my collection.

Do not show this letter to Helms as I have given you these facts in confidence. If I can be of any further assistance to you I will be very glad to do so. I have *not* as yet received "The Auk" for Oct, and do not know what is the matter. Please send me the Oct, no. and I will promptly send you the [illegible symbols possibly indicating $ and cents] for it.

Very truly yours,
Arthur T. Wayne

APPENDIX 2

Known Specimens of Imperial Woodpeckers

DATE	MAP	INSTITUTION*	CATALOG #	SEX	LATITUDE/ LONGITUDE
18910110		AMNH	56596(?)	F	30°05'N/108°43'W
18920125	X	AMNH	56820	M	29°35'N/108°25'W
18920125	X	AMNH	56901	F	29°35'N/108°25'W
18920129	X	AMNH	56902	M	29°35'N/108°25'W
18920129	X	AMNH	56903	F	29°35'N/108°25'W
18920516	X	AMNH	488387	F	20°36'N/104°41'W
18920518	X	AMNH	488386	M	20°36'N/104°41'W
18920520	X	AMNH	488385	M	20°36'N/104°41'W
18921215	X	AMNH	488388	F	20°36'N/104°41'W
19040220	X	AMNH	363844615	F	23°40'N/105°54'W
19191220		AMNH	819553	M	30°02'N/108°25'W
19211225		AMNH	958881	F	30°02'N/108°25'W
19211227		AMNH	188857	F	30°02'N/108°25'W
19211227		AMNH	188858	F	30°02'N/108°25'W
19340629		AMNH	300158	F	

LOCATION	STATE	COLLECTOR	TYPE	NOTES
Rancheria de los Apaches at 2020 m	SO	Robinette, F.	skin	6620' alt. (Allen 1893)
Col. Chuhuichupa	CH	Meeds	skin	
Col. Chuhuichupa	CH	Meeds	skin	
Col. Chuhuichupa	CH	Meeds	skin	
Col. Chuhuichupa	CH	Meeds	skin	
Sierra de Juanacatlán	JA	Buller, A. C.	skin	Near Mascota? (Salvin and Godman 1888–97)
Sierra de Juanacatlán	JA	Buller, A. C.	skin	Near Mascota? (Salvin and Godman 1888–97)
Sierra de Juanacatlán	JA	Buller, A. C.	skin	Near Mascota? (Salvin and Godman 1888–97)
Sierra de Juanacatlán	JA	Buller, A. C.	skin	Near Mascota? (Salvin and Godman 1888–97)
125 m w. of Durango	DU	Worthen, C. K.	skin	Near crest of sierra at 7465'
Mound Valley (10 mi. s. of Col. Pacheco)	CH	Brown, W. W.	skin	
Mound Valley	CH	Brown, W. W.	skin	
Mound Valley	CH	Brown, W. W.	skin	
Mound Valley	CH	Brown, W. W.	skin	
			skin	Sent by customs in El Paso, TX; gift to G. C. Graves

(continued next page)

DATE	MAP	INSTITUTION*	CATALOG #	SEX	LATITUDE/ LONGITUDE
?		AMNH		M	
?		AMNH	142885	F	
18360900		ANSP	19612	F	
		ANSP	19613	M	
		ANSP	19614	F	
		ANSP	19615	M	
19020700	X	ANSP	39484	M	29°58'N/108°28'W
19020700	X	ANSP	39485	F	29°58'N/108°28'W
18820100		BMNH	18888563	M	23°44'N/104°34'W
18820100	X	BMNH	18888562	F	23°46'N/105°15'W
18820215	X	BMNH	18983102486	M	23°46'N/105°15'W
18820215	X	BMNH	18983102487	F	23°46'N/105°15'W
18820100		BMNH		F	23°46'N/105°15'W
18820100		BMNH		M	23°46'N/105°15'W
18320000		BMNH	18888560	F	21°40'N/103°55'W
18320000		BMNH	18888561	M	21°40'N/103°55'W
18320000		BMNH	1988216	M	21°40'N/103°55'W
19070000		Bob Howard		M	unknown
19070000		Bob Howard		F	unknown
19050905		CMNH	118047	M	30°02'N/108°25'W
19260000	X	CU	42232	U	25°58'N/107°02'W
19030000	X	DENV	27341	M	28°29'N/107°31'W
19030000	X	DENV	27342	F	28°25'N/107°21'W
19230500	X	DENV	9790	F	29°09'N/108°22'W
		DENV	33780	M	

LOCATION	STATE	COLLECTOR	TYPE	NOTES
			skin	"On display in exposition"; likely the same as mounted male seen in photo by H. S. Rice taken in March 1933 (AMNH Negative #103797)
	DU	Sanford, L. C.	skin	
		Taylor, J.	skin	Rivoli collection; immature?
			skin	Rivoli collection
			skin	Rivoli collection
			skin	Rivoli collection
Col. García	CH	Cluff, H. A.	skin	Purchased by Cluff
Col. García	CH	Cluff, H. A.	skin	Purchased by Cluff
La Ciudad	DU		skin	
La Ciudad	DU		skin	
La Ciudad	DU		skin	
La Ciudad	DU		skin	
ca. La Ciudad	DU		skin	Mounted specimen on display NHM, London
ca. La Ciudad	DU		skin	Mounted speciman on display NHM, London
Sierra Bolaños	JA		skin	Syntype; J. Gould
Sierra Bolaños	JA		skin	Syntype; J. Gould
ca. Bolaños?	JA		skin	
Chihuahua, México	CH		mount	Skeleton in USNM collection? Not found
Chihuahua, México	CH		mount	Mounted with previous specimen
Mound Valley	CH	Brown, W. W.	skin	From MCZ (#302891)
between Hidalgo de Parral and Culiacan	DU	Vickers, W. A.	skull	10,500' in virgin pine forest; collected between 1926–28
ca. Miñaca	CH	Harlow, E. G.	skin	Winter 1903–4
ca. Miñaca	CH	Harlow, E. G.	skin	Winter 1903–4
ca. Miñaca	CH	Lethbridge, J. A. M.	skin	
			skin	

(continued next page)

DATE	MAP	INSTITUTION*	CATALOG #	SEX	LATITUDE/ LONGITUDE
19020600		FMNH	12645	M	29°10'N/107°45'W
19020600		FMNH	12648	M	29°10'N/107°45'W
19020600		FMNH	12649	F	29°10'N/107°45'W
19020609	X	FMNH	12646	F	29°10'N/107°45'W
19020612	X	FMNH	12650	M	29°10'N/107°45'W
19020616	X	FMNH	12647	M	29°10'N/107°45'W
19020624	X	FMNH	12638	M	29°10'N/107°45'W
19040806	X	FMNH	15946	M	23°49'N/105°20'W
19040825	X	FMNH	15947	F	23°49'N/105°20'W
19040903	X	FMNH	15942	M	23°42'N/105°40'W
19040903	X	FMNH	15943	F	23°49'N/105°20'W
19040903	X	FMNH	15944	M	23°49'N/105°20'W
19040904	X	FMNH	15945	M	23°49'N/105°20'W
19090718	X	FMNH	124532	M	30°06'N/108°26'W
19090718	X	FMNH	124533	F	30°06'N/108°26'W
19090718	X	FMNH	124534	M	30°06'N/108°26'W
19060000		LAM	944	M	30°29'N/108°34'W
19060000		LAM	944	F	30°29'N/108°34'W
19120000	X	LAM	1497	M	24°30'N/105°02'W
19380331	X	LSUMZ	42916	M	23°39'N/105°44'W
18840500	X	MCZ	224288	M	28°21'N/107°52'W
18880707		MCZ	224289	M	28°16'N/108°18'W
18880707		MCZ	224290	F	28°16'N/108°18'W
19030401	X	MCZ	110980	F	29°58'N/108°28'W

LOCATION	STATE	COLLECTOR	TYPE	NOTES
Babicora?	CH	Breninger, G. F.		Head and wing; immature; slight red on crown
Babicora?	CH	Breninger, G. F.	skin	
Babicora?	CH	Breninger, G. F.	skin	
Babicora	CH	Breninger, G. F.	skin	L 22.5" wing 12.5" from label
Babicora	CH	Breninger, G. F.	skin	
Babicora	CH	Breninger, G. F.	skin	
Babicora	CH	Breninger, G. F.	skin	
Coyotes	DU		skin	Iris cream yellow
Coyotes	DU		skin	Iris lemon yellow
Coyotes	DU		skin	Iris lemon yellow
Coyotes	DU		mount	
Coyotes	DU		skin	Iris lemon yellow
Coyotes	DU		mount	
Col. Pacheco	CH	Kimball, H. H.	skin	
Col. Pacheco	CH	Kimball, H. H.	skin	
Col. Pacheco	CH	Kimball, H. H.	skin	Immature; slight red on crown
35 mi. w. of Casas Grandes (Sierra Madre)	SO-CH	Neely, W. L.	skin	Bill = 91 mm (gap = 91 mm); TL = 450.5 mm; relaxed from mount
35 mi. w. of Casas Grandes	SO-CH	Neely, W. L.	skin	Bill = 79.5 mm (gap = 84.5 mm); TL = 447.5 mm; relaxed from mount
Mtns. of Durango	DU	Hale, W. J.	skin	Bill = 77.5 mm (gap = 89 mm); TL = 529.5 mm; relaxed from mount
4 mi. w. of Nievero (La Ciudad); 8000'	DU	Lamb, C. C.	skin	Rec'd from MLZ (#20608); male of a pair atop a dead pine; three seen
Temochíc	CH	McLeod, R. R.	skin	Crest of Sierra Madre near villlage of Temochic, Mex.; alt. 8000'; iris red
Pinos Altos	CH	Frazar, M. A.	skin	
Pinos Altos	CH	Frazar, M. A.	skin	
Col. García	CH	Barber, C. W.	skin	

(continued next page)

DATE	MAP	INSTITUTION*	CATALOG #	SEX	LATITUDE/ LONGITUDE
19050911		MCZ	114748	F	30°02'N/108°25'N
19050902		MCZ	302879	F	30°02'N/108°25'W
19050904		MCZ	302886	M	30°02'N/108°25'N
19050905		MCZ	302883	F	30°02'N/108°25'N
19050905		MCZ	302887	F	30°02'N/108°25'N
19050906		MCZ	302888	F	30°02'N/108°25'N
19050915	X	MCZ	302881	F	29°35'N/108°25'W
19050916	X	MCZ	114747	M	29°35'N/108°25'W
19050917	X	MCZ	302882	F	29°35'N/108°25'W
19050918	X	MCZ	302884	F	29°35'N/108°25'W
19030401	X	MCZ	110979	M	29°58'N/108°28'W
		MCZ	237909	F	
		MCZ	237908		
	X	MCZ	333080	F	27°52'N/107°49'W
19370517	/	MLZ	18444	M	26°06'N/107°04'W
19370721	X	MLZ	19067	M	26°28'N/106°28'W
19380331	X	MLZ	20609	F	23°39'N/105°44'W
19410611	X	MLZ	28875	M	22°32'N/104°47'W
19470728	X	MLZ	46336	F	23°28'N/104°38'W
19470728	X	MLZ	46338	M	23°28'N/104°38'W

LOCATION	STATE	COLLECTOR	TYPE	NOTES
Mound Valley (10 mi. s. of Col. Pacheco)	CH	Brown, W. W.	skin	
Mound Valley	CH	Brown, W. W.	skin	
Mound Valley	CH	Brown, W. W.	skin	
Mound Valley	CH	Brown, W. W.	skin	
Mound Valley	CH	Brown, W. W.	skin	
Mound Valley	CH	Brown, W. W.	skin	
ca. Col. Chuhuichupa	CH	Brown, W. W.	skin	
ca. Col. Chuhuichupa	CH	Brown, W. W.	skin	Immature; incomplete red crown
ca. Col. Chuhuichupa	CH	Brown, W. W.	skin	
ca. Col. Chuhuichupa	CH	Brown, W. W.	skin	
ca. Col. García	CH	Barber C. W.	skin	
	CH			April 14, no year
	CH			April 14, no year; no head
Jesus María	CH	McLeod, R. R.	head	Iris golden yellow "Shot / 86"?
10,000' Valle Imperial, Cerro Mohinora	CH	Moore, R. T.	skin	"Two seen, two heard."
9000' Laguna Juanota	CH	Lamb, C. C.	skin	"High on a tall dead pine. Six seen, many heard."
4 mi. w. Nievero (La Ciudad); 8000'	DU	Lamb, C. C.		Female of collected pair; three seen
10 mi. w. of Santa Teresa; 5500'	NY	Lamb, C. C.	skin	"On top of a dead pine. Four seen." (three ivory-billed and four imperials)*
8,000' mtns.; 50 mi. s. of Durango	DU	Lamb, C. C.	skin	"On top snag of a dead pine. Four seen."
8,000' mtns.; 50 mi. s. of Durango	DU	Lamb, C. C.	skin	"On top snag of a dead pine. Four seen." Exch to MNHUK #43123

(continued next page)

*Since ivory-billed woodpeckers do not occur in the range of the imperial, we think the best interpretation of this specimen notation is that the observer saw four imperials and three pale-billed woodpeckers (*Campephilus guatemalensis*) together on a snag.

DATE	MAP	INSTITUTION*	CATALOG #	SEX	LATITUDE/ LONGITUDE
		NNHM		M	
19030000	X	ROM	45875	M	29°58'N/108°28'W
19030000	X	ROM	45876	F	29°58'N/108°28'W
19030000	x	ROM	45873	U	29°58'N/108°28'W
19040220	X	ROM	45874	F	24°00'N/106°02'W
?		SDNHM	13448	M	23°43'N/104°31'W
?	X	SDNHM	29855	M	29°38'N/108°37'W
19050905		UCLA		M	30°02'N/108°25'W
19050910		UCLA		F	30°02'N/108°25'W
18920100	X	UMMZ	21966	M	21°34'N/103°56'W
18920100	X	UMMZ	21967	F	21°34'N/103°56'W
18920800	X	UMMZ	29214	F	21°34'N/103°56'W
18920800	X	UMMZ	29215	M	21°34'N/103°56'W
18980223		UMMZ	29217	M	
18980228		UMMZ	29216	F	
	X	UMMZ	21473	F	21°39'N/103°56'W
	X	UMMZ	29213	F	21°34'N/103°56'W
		UMMZ	121930	M	
		UMMZ	121931	M	
		UMMZ	121933	F	
19020000		UNAM		M	
18860700	X	USNM	109524	F	29°57'N/108°50'W
18901200	X	USNM	1464	F	30°22'N/108°33'W

LOCATION	STATE	COLLECTOR	TYPE	NOTES
			mount	Adult; label reads Florida
ca. Col. García	CH	Cluff, H. A.	skin	
ca. Col. García	CH	Cluff, H. A.	skin	
ca. Col. García	CH	Cluff, H. A.	skin	Immature
125 mi. w. of Durango; 7465' at summit	DU	Andros, F. W.	skin	Formerly C. K. Worthen coll.
Sierra de Durango	DU	Huey, L. M.	skin	Relaxed from mount; received from Inst. de Biologia, Mexico, D.F.
Candeleria Pk., 15 mi. w. Chuhuichupa	CH	Fuelscher, W. M.	skin	Iris yellow; catalogued 1949–50; mapped as Candelaria Peak
Mound Valley	CH	Brown, W. W.	skin	From MCZ
Mound Valley	CH	Brown, W. W.	skin	From MCZ
Sierra Bolaños	JA	Moore, A. J.		No longer in UMMZ; location unknown
Sierra Bolaños	JA	Moore, A. J.		No longer in UMMZ; location unknown
Sierra Bolaños	JA	Moore, A. J.		
Sierra Bolaños	JA	Moore, A. J.?		No longer in UMMZ; exchanged; location unknown
	DU	Fisher, W. S.		
	DU	Fisher, W. S.		
ca. Bolaños	JA	Moore, A. J.		No longer in UMMZ; location unknown
Sierra Bolaños	JA	Moore, A. J.	mount	No longer in UMMZ; location unknown
		Allen, J. D.	skin	Immature; label erroneously reads Florida
		Allen, J. D.	skin	Label erroneously reads Florida
			skin	No label
"México"				On loan from FMNH (#12765)
Rio Bavispe; Sierra Huachinera	SO	Benson, H. C.	head	
Sierra Madre de Sonora	SO	Berlandier, L.	skull	Skull; fide J. A. Allen

(continued next page)

DATE	MAP	INSTITUTION*	CATALOG #	SEX	LATITUDE/LONGITUDE
18920723	X	USNM	155010	F	19°29'N/101°31'W
18921000	X	USNM	128441	M	19°41'N/101°59'W
18921000	X	USNM	128442	F	19°41'N/101°59'W
18921007	X	USNM	155011	M	19°41'N/101°59'W
18921009	X	USNM	155012	F	19°41'N/101°59'W
18921010	X	USNM	155013	F	19°41'N/101°59'W
18921010	X	USNM	155014	M	19°41'N/101°59'W
18921011	X	USNM	155015	M	19°41'N/101°59'W
18921011	X	USNM	155016	F	19°41'N/101°59'W
18980711	X	USNM	163923	M	23°46'N/105°15'W
18980711	X	USNM	163925	F	23°46'N/105°15'W
18980717	X	USNM	163926	F	23°46'N/105°15'W
18980721	X	USNM	163924	F	23°46'N/105°15'W
18990707	X	USNM	165505	M	29°58'N/108°28'W
18990707	X	USNM	165508	F	29°58'N/108°28'W
18990710	X	USNM	165507	F	29°58'N/108°28'W
18990712	X	USNM	165509	F	29°58'N/108°28'W
18990730	X	USNM	165506	M	29°58'N/108°28'W
19020301	X	USNM	188291	M	30°06'N/108°21'W
19030401	X	USNM	189839	F	29°58'N/108°28'W
19040224	X	USNM	187767	M	29°58'N/108°28'W
19040224	X	USNM	187768	F	29°58'N/108°30'W
19370915	X	USNM	344439	F	29°59'N/108°22'W
19370916	X	USNM	344440	F	29°59'N/108°22'W
19370916	X	USNM	344441	M	29°59'N/108°22'W
18921000	X	USNM	128443	F	19°41'N/101°59'W
No date		WFVZ		M	

LOCATION	STATE	COLLECTOR	TYPE	NOTES
Pátzcuaro	MI	Nelson, E. W.	skin	Immature
Nahuatzén	MI	Winton, G. B.	skin	
Nahuatzén	MI	Winton, G. B.	skin	
Nahuatzén	MI	Nelson, E. W.	skin	
Nahuatzén	MI	Nelson, E. W.	skin	
Nahuatzén	MI	Nelson, E. W.	skin	
Nahuatzén	MI	Nelson, E. W.	skin	
Nahuatzén	MI	Nelson, E. W.	skin	
Nahuatzén	MI	Nelson, E. W.	skin	
El Salto	DU	Nelson, E. W.	skin	
El Salto	DU	Nelson, E. W.	skin	
El Salto	DU	Nelson, E. W.	skin	
El Salto	DU	Nelson, E. W.	skin	
ca. Col. García	CH	Nelson, E. W.	skin	
ca. Col. García	CH	Nelson, E. W.	skin	
ca. Col. García	CH	Nelson, E. W.	skin	
ca. Col. García	CH	Nelson, E. W.	skin	
ca. Col. García	CH	Nelson, E. W.	skin	
ca. Col.García-Col. Pacheco	CH	Steiner, E.	skin	
ca. Col. García	CH	Barber, C. M.	skin	
5 mi. w. of Col. García	CH	Gaut, J. H.	skin	
15 mi. w. of Col. García	CH	Gaut, J. H.	skin	
15 mi. ne. of Col. García	CH	Castle, W.	skel.	Skeleton; trunk
15 mi. ne. of Col. García	CH	Castle, W.	skel.	Skeleton; trunk; humeri; tibia
15 mi. ne. of Col. García	CH	Castle, W.	skel.	Skeleton; whole
Nahuatzén	MI	Winton, G. B.	mount	
	CH		mount	Collected near Mormon settlement

(continued next page)

DATE	MAP	INSTITUTION*	CATALOG #	SEX	LATITUDE/ LONGITUDE
No date		WFVZ	18495	M	
19100602		YPM	58535		
19100602		YPM	58534		
19050914	X	ZIN	112329	F	29°35'N/108°25'W
19050916	X	ZIN	112330	M	29°35'N/108°25'W
		MADUG		M	
		SMF		M	
		MHNN	92.584		
		MHNN	92.584		
		MHNN	92.584		
		MHNC	21.01.0302	M	
		NML	D.3868	M	
		NML	D.3868a	F	
		NMW	44.736	M	
		NMW	44.735		
19050905		NMW	84.917		
19050914		NMW	84.917		
19050916	X	ZIN	112330	M	29°35'N/108°25'W
18990000		ZMB	51.146	F	
18990000		ZMB	51.145	M	
		ZMB	19265	F	
		SDM		M	
1936		KM	1936.2.1	M	

LOCATION	STATE	COLLECTOR	TYPE	NOTES
	CH		skin	Collected near Mormon settlement; relaxed from mount
Black Canyon	CH	Ledbetter, L. T.	skin	
Black Canyon	CH	Ledbetter, L. T.	skin	
Col. Chuhuichupa	CH	Brown, W. W.	skin	Received 1932; #108-932
Col. Chuhuichupa	CH	Brown, W. W.	skin	Received 1932; #108-932
	CO		skull	Skull with feathers
"Ciudad Durango"	DU		skin	"Collected in the nineteenth century."
		Borel, A.	skin	
		Borel, A.	skin	
		Borel, A.	skin	
		Borel, A.	skin	Donated from MHNN, 1922
			skin	Received in 1851 from 13th Earl of Derby; J. Gould syntypes?
			skin	Received in 1851 from 13th Earl of Derby; J. Gould syntypes?
			mount	Donation from F. Steinbacher 1885; bought from Forrer, CA
			skin	Donation from F. Steinbacher 1885; bought from Forrer, CA; relaxed mount
Mound Valley	CH	Brown, W. W.	skin	Purchased 1986/87 from Graf Seilern (Litschau, Austria); no. 11808
Chuhuichupa	CH	Brown, W. W.	skin	Purchased 1986/87 from Graf Seilern (Litschau, Austria); no. 11809
Col. Chuhuichupa	CH	Brown, W. W.	skin	Received 1932; #108-932
Sierra Madre	DU	Damm, F. C.	skin	·Collected "1899–1900"
Sierra Madre	DU	Damm, F. C.	skin	Collected "1899–1900"
			mount	
				No data
"probably Sonora, Mexico"	SO	Middling, H.	mount	"Were seen together in flight and both were killed in less than twenty-five minutes."

(continued next page)

DATE	MAP	INSTITUTION*	CATALOG #	SEX	LATITUDE/ LONGITUDE
1936		KM	1936.2.2	M	
1922		EUP		M	
1922		EUP		F	
		CMUTEP		M	
		CNUTEP		F	
		MWNH		M	
		MWNH		F	

DISPOSITION UNKNOWN

ca. 1940		NONE		U	27°16'N/107°51'W?
19271000		NONE		M	
19271000		NONE		F	

* INSTITUTION

AMNH	American Museum of Natural History, New York
ANSP	Academy of Natural Sciences, Philadelphia
BMNH	British Museum of Natural History, London
CMNH	Carnegie Museum of Natural History, Pittsburgh, PA
CMUTEP	Centennial Museum, University of Texas, El Paso
CU	Cornell University, Ithaca, New York
DENV	Denver Museum of Natural History
EUP	Edinboro University of Pennsylvania, Edinboro, PA
FMNH	Field Musuem of Natural History, Chicago
KM	Kingman Museum, Battle Creek, Michigan
LAM	Los Angeles County Museum of Natural History
LSUMZ	Louisiana State University Museum of Zoology
MADUG	Museo Alfredo Duges Universidad de Guanajuato, Mexico
MCZ	Museum of Comparative Zoology, Harvard, Cambridge, MA
MHNC	Musee d'histoire naturelle, La Chaux-de-Fonds, Switzerland
MHNN	Museum d'histoire naturelle, Neuchatel, Switzerland
MLZ	Moore Laboratory of Zoology, Occidental College, Los Angeles

LOCATION	STATE	COLLECTOR	TYPE	NOTES
"probably Sonora, Mexico"	SO	Middling, H.		
"Mexico"		Westcott, H. P.	mount	Gifted to EU in 1974 from Erie Public Museum; received at Erie Public Museum, July 13, 1922; possibly collected May 1922
"Mexico"		Westcott, H. P.	mount	Gifted to EU in 1974 from Erie Public Museum; received at Erie Public Museum, July 13, 1922; possibly collected May 1922
			mount	No data
			mount	No data
"Sierra Madre"			mount	From Sierra Madre (Mex.); donated by Ad. V. Hagen (Wiesbaden) in 1908
"Sierra Madre"			mount	From Sierra Madre (Mex.); donated by Ad. V. Hagen (Wiesbaden) in 1908
Rancho Campo Bonito	CH	Brady	spec.	(Williams 1984: 79)
Head of Rio Yaqui	SO	Grimes, C. W.	mount	(Grimes 1928); photo
Head of Rio Yaqui	SO	Palmer, D.	mount	(Grimes 1928); photo

MWNH	Museum Wiesbaden, Germany
NML	National Museum Liverpool, UK
NMW	Natural History Museum-Wien, Vienna, Austria
NNHM	Netherlands Natural History Museum, Leiden
ROM	Royal Ontario Musem, Toronto
SDM	State Darwin Museum, Moscow, Russia
SDNHM	San Diego Natural History Museum
SMF	Forschungsinstitut Senckenberg, Frankfurt, Germany
UCLA	University of California at Los Angeles
UMMZ	University of Michigan Museum of Zoology
UNAM	Universidad Autonoma de Mexico, Mexico City
USNM	U.S. National Museum, Smithsonian Institution, Washington DC
WFVZ	Western Foundation of Vertebrate Zoology, Camarillo, CA
YPM	Yale Peabody Museum, New Haven, CT
ZIN	Zoological Institute, St. Petersburg, Russia
ZMB	Museum fuer Naturkunde der Humboldt, Berlin, Germany

LITERATURE CITED

Allen, A. A. 1951. *Stalking birds with color camera*. Washington, DC: National Geographic Society.

Allen, A. A., and P. P. Kellogg. 1937. Recent observations on the ivory-billed woodpecker. *Auk* 54: 164–84.

Allen, J. A. 1876. On the decrease of birds in the United States. *Penn Monthly* (December): 931–44.

———. 1893. List of mammals and birds collected in northeastern Sonora and northwestern Chihuahua, Mexico, on the Lumholtz Archeological Expedition, 1890–1892. *Bull. Amer. Mus. Nat. Hist.* 5: 27–42.

Allen, R. P. 1952. *The whooping crane*. Research report 3. New York: National Audubon Society.

Allen, R. P., and A. Sprunt, Jr. 1936. The Carolina paroquet (*Conuropsis c. carolinensis*) in the Santee Swamp, South Carolina. Unpublished report. New York: National Association of Audubon Societies.

Askins, R. A. 2000. *Restoring North America's birds*. New Haven, CT: Yale University Press.

Audubon, J. J. 1842. *Birds of America*. Vol. 4. Philadelphia: Chevalier. Repr. New York: Dover, 1967.

———. 1929. *Journal of John James Audubon made during his trip to New Orleans in 1820–1821*. Cambridge, MA: Boston Historical Society.

Baird, S. F., J. Cassin, and G. N. Lawrence. 1860. *The birds of North America: The descriptions of species based chiefly on the collections in the museum of the Smithsonian Institution*. Philadelphia: Lippincott.

Baker, R. H. 1958. Nest of the military macaw in Durango. *Auk* 75: 98.

Bangs, O. 1899. The hummingbirds of the Santa Marta region of Colombia. *Auk* 16 (2): 134–39.

Banko, W. E. 1960. *The Trumpeter Swan: Its history, habits, and population in the United States*. North American Fauna. Monograph no. 63.

Barbour, T. 1943. *Cuban ornithology*. Mem. Nuttall Ornithol. Club. Monograph no. 9.

Barrow, M. V., Jr. 2000. The specimen dealer: Entrepreneurial natural history in America's gilded age. *J. Hist. Biol.* 33: 493–534.

Bendire, C. 1895. Life histories of North American birds. *Spec. Bull. U.S. Nat. Mus.* 3: 42–45, 102–7.

Bennett, E. L., and M. T. Gumal. 2001. The interrelationships of commercial logging, hunting, and wildlife in Sarawak. In *The cutting edge: Conserving wildlife in logged tropical forest*, ed. R. A. Fimbel, A. Grajal, and J. Robinson, 360–74. New York: Columbia University Press.

Bennett, W. C., and R. M. Zingg. 1935. *The Tarahumara*. Chicago: University of Chicago Press.

Bergtold, W. H. 1906. Concerning the thick-billed parrot. *Auk* 23: 425–28.

Betancourt, J. L. 1990. Late Quaternary biogeography of the Colorado Plateau. In *Packrat middens: The last 40,000 years of biotic change*, ed. J. L. Betancourt, T. R. Van Devender, and P. S. Martin, 259–92. Tucson: University of Arizona Press.

Beyer, G. G. 1900. The ivory-billed woodpecker in Louisiana. *Auk* 17: 97–99.

Bishop, W. C. 1998. *Aves de Durango*. Durango, Mexico: Impresora Magasa.

Boardman, G. A. 1885. The big woodpeckers. *Forest and Stream* 24 (20): 388.

Brenner, A. 1943. *The wind that swept Mexico: The history of the Mexican revolution, 1910–1942*. New York: Harper and Brothers.

Brewster, W. 1881. With the birds on a Florida river. *Bull. Nuttall Ornithol. Club* 6: 38–44.

Brodkorb, P. 1971. Catalogue of fossil birds. Pt. 4. Columbiformes through Piciformes. *Bull. Fla. State Mus.* 15 (4): 163–266.

Brown, D. E., ed. 1983. *The wolf in the Southwest: The making of an endangered species*. Tucson: University of Arizona Press.

———. 1985a. *Arizona game birds*. Tucson: University of Arizona Press.

———.π 1985b. *The grizzly in the Southwest*. Norman: University of Oklahoma Press.

Brown, D. E., F. W. Reichenbacher, and S. E. Franson. 1998. *A classification of North American biotic communities*. Salt Lake City: University of Utah Press.

Brown, D. E., P. J. Unmack, and T. C. Brennan. 2007. Digitized map of the biotic communities for plotting and comparing distributions of North American animals. *Southwest. Nat.* 52 (4): 610–16 and fold-out map.

Bryant, H. 1859. [Birds observed in east Florida, south of St. Augustine.] *Proc. Boston Soc. Nat. Hist.* 7: 5–21.

Bull, E. L., and J. A. Jackson. 1995. Pileated woodpecker (*Dryocopus pileatus*). In *The birds of North America*, ed. A. Poole and F. Gill. Monograph no. 148. Philadelphia: Academy of Natural Sciences; Washington, DC: American Ornithologists' Union.

Burleigh, T. D. 1958. *Georgia birds*. Norman: University of Oklahoma Press.

Carlton, L. A. 1922. *History of a hunting trip in Sierra Madres, northern Mexico, August 21 to October 1, 1922*. Houston, TX: privately printed.

Carmony, N. B., and D. E. Brown. 1983. *Mexican game trails*. Norman: University of Oklahoma Press.

Cassin, J. 1856. *Illustrations of the birds of California, Texas, Oregon, British and Russian America*. Philadelphia: Lippincott. Facsimile reproduction by Austin: Texas State Historical Association, 1991.

Catesby, M. 1731. *Natural history of Carolina, Florida and the Bahama Islands*. Vol. 1. London: privately printed.

Ceballos, G., P. Balvanera, S. González, P. Jenkins, G. Nelson, R. Benitez, C. Flores, C. Galindo, F. Bunnell, and S. Valencia. 1992. *Estudio de Especies Amenazadas y en Peligro de Extinción*. Informe final. Mexico City: Centro de Ecología, UNAM.

Ceballos-Lascurain, H. 1987. Reporte de la expedicion cientifica internacional en busqueda de pajaro carpintero imperial (*Campephilus imperialis*) en la Sierra Madre Occidental de Durango en el mes de Abril de 1987. Unpubl. ms.

Chapman, F. M. 1930. Notes on the plumage of North American birds: Ivory-billed woodpecker. *Bird-Lore* 32 (4): 265–67, 307.

Clark, S. C. 1885. The ivory-billed woodpecker in Florida. *Forest and Stream* 24 (19): 367.

Cokinos, C. 2000. *Hope is the thing with feathers*. New York: Tarcher/Putnam.

Collar, N. J., L. P. Gonzaga, N. Krabbe, A. Madroño-Nieto, L. G. Naranjo, T. A. Parker, and D. C. Wege. 1992. *Threatened birds of the Americas: ICBP/IUCN red data book*. Cambridge, UK: International Council for Bird Preservation.

Collinson, J. M. 2007. Video analysis of the escape flight of pileated woodpecker *Dryocopus pileatus*: Does the ivory-billed woodpecker *Campephilus principalis* persist in continental North America? *BMC Biology* 5: 8 www.biomedcentral.com/1741-7007/5/8.

Cooke, W. W. 1888. Report on bird migration in the Mississippi Valley in the years 1884 and 1885. *U.S. Dept. Agric., Bull. Div. Econ. Ornith.* 2: 127–28.

Cory, C. B. 1892. Remarks on a collection of birds made by Wilmot W. Brown, Jr., on Mona and Porto Rico during February and a part of March. *Auk* 9 (3): 228–29.

Coues, E. 1887. *Key to North American birds*. Boston: Estes and Lauriat.

———. 1903. *Key to North American birds*. 5th ed. Boston: Page.

Critchfield, W. B., and E. L. Little, Jr. 1966. *Geographic distribution of the pines of the world*. Washington, DC: U.S. Department of Agriculture, Forest Service.

D., W. A. 1885. The great woodpecker. *Forest and Stream* 24 (22): 427.

DeBano, L. F., P. F. Ffolliott, A. Ortego-Rubio, G. J. Gottfried, R. H. Hamre, and C. B. Edminster, tech. coords. 1995. *Biodiversity and management of the Madrean Archipelago: The sky islands of southwestern United States and northwestern Mexico. Sept. 19–23, 1994*. Tucson, AZ. General Technical Report RM-GTR-264. Fort Collins, CO: U.S. Department of Agriculture, Forest Service, Rocky Mountain Forest and Range Experiment Station.

Dennis, J. V. 1948. A last remnant of ivory-billed woodpeckers in Cuba. *Auk* 65: 497–507.

———. 1967. The ivory-bill flies still. *Audubon* 69 (6): 38–44.

———. 1984. Tale of two woodpeckers. *Living Bird Quarterly* 3: 18–21.

Di Peso, C. C. 1974. *Casas Grandes: A fallen trading center of the Gran Chichimeca*. Series 9. Dragoon, AZ: Amerind Foundation.

Dixon, R. D., and V. A. Saab. 2000. Black-backed woodpecker (*Picoides arcticus*). In *The birds of North America*, ed. A. Poole and F. Gill. Monograph no. 509. Philadelphia: Birds of North America.

Douglas, M. W., R. A. Maddox, K. Howard, and S. Reyes. 1993. The Mexican monsoon. *J. Climate* 6 (8): 1665–77.

Eastman, W. 1958. Ten year search for the ivory-billed woodpecker. *Atl. Nat.* 13 (4): 216–28.

Elliott, C. N. 1932. Feathers of the Okefenokee. *Am. Forests* 38 (4): 202–6, 253.

Ellis, J. B. 1917. Forty years ago and more. *Oologist* 34: 2–4.

Fa, J., D. Currie, and J. Meeuwig. 2003. Bushmeat and food security in the Congo Basin: Linkages between wildlife and people's future. *Environ. Conserv.* 30 (1): 71–78.

Fimbel, R. A., A. Grajal, and J. Robinson. 2001. Logging and wildlife in the tropics: Impacts and options for conservation. In *The cutting edge: Conserving wildlife in logged tropical forest*, ed. R. A. Fimbel, A. Grajal, and J. Robinson, 667–95. New York: Columbia University Press.

Fitzpatrick, J. W. 2002. *Acoustic search for the ivory-billed woodpecker in the Pearl River Wildlife Management Area and the Bogue Chitto National Wildlife Refuge, Louisiana*. Final report, May 31, 2002, Cornell Laboratory of Ornithology.

Fitzpatrick, J. W., M. Lammertink, M. D. Luneau, Jr., T. W. Gallagher, B. R. Harrison, G. M. Sparling, K. V. Rosenberg, et al. 2005. Ivory-billed woodpecker (*Campephilus principalis*) persists in continental North America. *Science* 308: 1460–62.

Fleischer, R. C., J. J. Kirchman, J. P. Dumbacher, L. Bevier, D. Dove, N. C. Rotzel, S. V. Edwards, M. Lammertink, K. J. Miglia, and W. S. Moore. 2006. Mid-Pleistocene divergence of Cuban and North American ivory-billed woodpeckers. *Biol. Lett.* www.hmnh.harvard.edu/ivorybilled.pdf. doi:10.1098/rsbl.2006.0490.

Fleming, R. L., and R. H. Baker. 1963. Notes on the birds of Durango, Mexico. *Publ. Mus. Michigan State Univ. Biol. Ser.* 2 (5): 273–304.

Friedman, H., L. Griscom, and R. T. Moore. 1957. *Distributional check-list of the birds of Mexico: Part 2*. Berkeley, CA: Cooper Ornithological Society.

Gallagher, T. 2005. *The grail bird*. New York: Houghton Mifflin.

Gallina, S. 1981. Forest ecosystems of northwestern Mexico. In *Deer biology, habitat requirements, and management in western North America*, ed. P. F. Ffolliott and S. Gallina, 54–55. Mexico City: Instituto de Ecología.

Gallizioli, S., S. Levy, and J. Levy. 1967. Can the masked bobwhite be saved from extinction? *Audubon Field Notes* 2: 571–75.

Gaut, J. H. 1904. *[Field notes] in guide to the field reports of the United States Fish and Wildlife Service. 1860–1961 ca*, compiler, W. E. Cox, folder 23, box 124, series 3, Special Reports no. 4, Archives and Special Collections, Chihuahua, Mexico. Washington DC: Smithsonian Institution.

Goldman, E. A. 1951. Biological investigations in Mexico. *Smithsonian Misc. Coll.* 115: 1–476.

Goldman, E. A., and R. T. Moore. 1945. The biotic provinces of Mexico. *J. Mammal.* 26: 347–60.

Gosse, P. H. 1859. *Letters from Alabama (U.S.) chiefly relating to natural history*. London: Morgan and Chase. Repr. Tuscaloosa: University of Alabama Press, 1993.

Gould, J. 1832. *Picus imperialis*. *Pr. Comm. Sc. Zool. Soc.* 2: 140.

Grigera, D., C. Ubeda, and S. Cali. 1994. Caracterización ecologica de la assamblea de tetrápodos del Parque Nacional Nahuel Huapi, Argentina. *Rev. Chil. Hist. Nat.* 67: 273–98.

Grimes, C. W. 1928. A five day hunt in Mexico. *Outdoor Life*, March.

Griscom, L. 1933. Notes on the collecting trip of M. Abbot Frazar in Sonora and Chihuahua for William Brewster. *Auk* 50: 54–58.

Hahn, P. 1963. *Where is that vanished bird?* Toronto: Royal Ontario Museum and University of Toronto Press.

Hargrave, L. L. 1939. Bird bones from abandoned Indian dwellings in Arizona and Utah. *Condor* 41: 206–10.

Hasbrouck, E. M. 1891. The present status of the ivory-billed woodpecker (*Campephilus principalis*). *Auk* 8: 174–86.

Hibben, F. C. 1975. *Kiva art of the Anasazi at Pottery Mound*. Las Vegas, NV: KC.

Hill, G. 2007. *Ivorybill hunters: The search for proof in a flooded wilderness*. New York: Oxford University Press.

Hill, G. E., D. J. Mennill, B. W. Rolek, T. L. Hicks, and K. A. Swanson. 2006. Evidence suggesting that ivory-billed woodpeckers (*Campephilus principalis*) exist in Florida. *Avian Conservation and Ecology—Ecologie et conservation des oiseaux* 1 (3): 2. www.ace-eco.org/vol1/iss3/art2/.

Hitchcock, F. H. 1890. Capture of a second specimen of the Hooded Warbler in Massachusetts. *Auk* 7 (4): 407.

Hoose, P. 2004. *The race to save the lord god bird*. New York: Melanie Kroupa Books; Farrar, Straus, and Giroux.

Howell, S. N. G., and S. Webb. 1995. *A guide to the birds of Mexico and northern Central America*. New York: Oxford University Press.

Jackson, J. A. 2002. Ivory-billed woodpecker (*Campephilus principalis*). In *The birds of North America*, ed. A. Poole and F. Gill. Monograph no. 71. Philadelphia: Birds of North America.

———. 2004. *In search of the ivory-billed woodpecker*. Washington, DC: Smithsonian Books.

———. 2006. Ivory-billed woodpecker (*Campephilus principalis*): Hope and the interfaces of science, conservation, and politics. *Auk* 123: 1–15.

Kilham, L. 1972. Habits of the crimson-crested woodpecker in Panama. *Wilson Bull.* 84: 28–47.

———. 1976. Winter foraging and associated behavior of pileated woodpeckers in Georgia and Florida. *Auk* 93: 15–24.

Kline, H. A. 1886. Ivory-billed woodpecker. *Forest and Stream* 26 (9): 163.

———. 1887. Florida bird notes. *Forest and Stream* 28 (3): 43–44.

Knight, A. 1986. *The Mexican revolution*. 2 vols. Cambridge: Cambridge University Press.

Koford, C. B. 1953. *The California condor*. Research Report 4. New York: National Audubon Society.

Lamb, C. R. 1947. Field Notes. Housed at Occidental College, Los Angeles, CA.

Lamb, G. R. 1957. *The ivory-billed woodpecker in Cuba*. Research Report 1. New York: Pan-American Section, International Committee for Bird Preservation.

Lammertink, J. M. 1992. Search for ivory-billed woodpecker *Campephilus principalis* in Cuba. *Dutch Bird* 14: 170–73.

———. 1995. No more hope for the ivory-billed woodpecker *Campephilus principalis*. *Cotinga* 3: 45–47.

———. 2004. Grouping and cooperative breeding in the great slaty woodpecker. *Condor* 106: 309–19.

Lammertink, M., and A. R. Estrada. 1995. Status of the ivory-billed woodpecker *Campephilus principalis* in Cuba: Almost certainly extinct. *Bird Conserv. Int.* 5: 53–59.

Lammertink, J. M., and R. L. Otto. 1997. Report on fieldwork in the Rio Bavispe/ Sierra Tabaco area of northern Sonora in November–December 1996 (with a proposal for a larger conservation zone in the northern Sonora/Chihuahua border area). Unpubl. ms. The Netherlands: Institute for Systematics and Population Biology (Zoological Museum), University of Amsterdam.

Lammertink, J. M., J. A. Rojas-Tome, F. M. Casillas-Orona, and R. L. Otto. 1996. Status and conservation of old-growth forests and endemic birds in the pine-oak zone of the Sierra Madre Occidental, Mexico. *Verslagen en Technische Gegevens* 69: 1–89. The Netherlands: Institute for Systematics and Population Biology (Zoological Museum), University of Amsterdam.

Laurent, P. 1906. Bird notes from a Florida porch. *Bird Lore* 8: 67.

———. 1917. My ivory-billed woodpeckers. *Oologist* 34: 65–67.

Lea, R. B., and E. P. Edwards. 1950. Notes on birds of the Lake Patzcuaro region, Michoacan, Mexico. *Condor* 52: 260–71.

Leonard, D. L., Jr. 2001. Three-toed woodpecker (*Picoides tridactylus*). In *The birds of North America*, ed. A. Poole and F. Gill. Monograph no. 588. Philadelphia: Birds of North America.

Leopold, A. 1933. *Game management.* New York: Charles Scribner's Sons.

———. 1942. ca. Biotic land-use. In *Aldo Leopold: For the health of the land; Previously unpublished essays and other writings,* ed. J. B. Callicott and E. T. Freyfogle, 199. Washington, DC: Island, 1999.

———. 1949. *A sand county almanac and sketches here and there.* New York: Oxford University Press. Repr. 1970.

Leopold, A. S. 1959. *Wildlife of Mexico: The game birds and mammals.* Berkeley: University of California Press.

Lewis, J. C. 1995. Whooping crane (*Grus americana*). In *The birds of North America,* ed. A. Poole and F. Gill. Monograph no. 153. Philadelphia: Academy of Natural Sciences; Washington, DC: American Ornithologists' Union.

Lowery, G. H., Jr. 1974. *Louisiana birds.* 3rd ed. Baton Rouge: Louisiana State University Press.

Lumholtz, C. 1902. *Unknown Mexico.* 2 vols. New York: Charles Scribner's Sons.

Machado, M. A., Jr. 1981. *The north Mexican cattle industry, 1910–1975.* College Station: Texas A&M University Press.

Marshall, 1957. *Birds of pine-oak woodland in southern Arizona and adjacent Mexico.* Pacific Coast Avifauna. Monograph no. 32. Berkeley: Cooper Ornithological Society.

Mason, D. J., and J.-M. Thiollay. 2001. Tropical forestry and the conservation of neotropical birds. In *The cutting edge: Conserving wildlife in logged tropical forest,* ed. R. A. Fimbel, A. Grajal, and J. Robinson, 167–91. New York: Columbia University Press.

Maynard, C. J. 1881. *The birds of eastern North America.* Newtonville, MA: Maynard.

Mayr, E., and L. L. Short. 1970. *Species taxa of North American birds: A contribution to comparative systematics.* Publ. Nuttall Ornithol. Club. Monograph no. 9.

McIlhenny, E. A. 1941. The passing of the ivory-billed woodpecker. *Auk* 58: 582–84.

McKelvey, K. S., K. B. Aubry, and M. K. Schwartz. 2008. Using anecdotal occurrence data for rare or elusive species: The illusion of reality and a call for evidentiary standards. *BioScience* 58 (6): 549–55.

Mee, A., and L. S. Hall, eds. 2007. *California condors in the 21st century.* Series in Ornithology 2. Cambridge, MA: Nuttall Ornithological Club; Washington, DC: American Ornithologists' Union.

Miller, A. H., H. Friedmann, L. Griscom, and R. T. Moore 1957. *Distributional check-list of the birds of Mexico: Part 2.* Pacific Coast Avifauna. Monograph no. 33. Berkeley: Cooper Ornithological Society.

Moreno Bonilla, A. 1938. Necesidad de proteger nuestras aves. *Mem. Soc. Cubana Hist. Nat. "Felipe Poey"* 12: 181–90.

Moseley, E. L. 1928. The abundance of woodpeckers and other birds in northeastern Louisiana. *Wilson Bull.* 40: 115–16.

Nehrling, H. 1882. List of birds observed at Houston, Harris Co., Texas, and in the counties Montgomery, Galveston and Ford Bend. *Bull. Nuttall Ornithol. Club* 7 (3): 166–75.

Nelson, E. W. 1898. The imperial ivory-billed woodpecker, *Campephilus imperialis* (Gould). *Auk* 15 (3): 216–23.

Newton, I. 1979. *Population ecology of raptors.* Berkhamsted, UK: Poyser.

———. ed. 1989. *Lifetime reproduction in birds.* London, UK: Academic.

Nocedal, J., X. Vega, M. A. Cruz, A. Lafon, and A. Navarro. 2005. The status of the imperial woodpecker (*Campephilus imperialis*) habitats in western Mexico and recent reports. Abstract of paper presented at the Large Woodpecker Symposium, Brinkley, AR.

Nuttall, T. 1832. *A manual of the ornithology of the United States and of Canada*. New York: Arno.

Oberholser, H. C. 1974. *The bird life of Texas*. Austin: University of Texas Press.

Ojeda, V. 2003. Magellanic woodpecker frugivory and predation on a lizard. *Wilson Bull*. 115: 208–10.

———. 2004. Breeding biology and social behaviour of Magellanic woodpeckers (*Campephilus magellanicus*) in Argentine Patagonia. *Eur. J. Wildlife Res*. 50: 18–24.

Ojeda, V. S., and M. L. Chazarreta. 2006. Provisioning of Magellanic woodpecker (*Campephilus magellanicus*) nestlings with vertebrate prey. *Wilson J. Ornithol*. 118 (2): 251–54.

Otto, R. 2003. Threatened wildlife and old-growth forest survey of the Arroyo Durango, Sierra Madre Occidental, Durango, Mexico. Unpubl. ms. A joint project by PROSIMA, A. C. and BirdLife International.

Pearson, T. G. 1932. Protection of the ivory-billed woodpecker. *Bird Lore* 34 (4): 300–301.

———. 1933. Woodpeckers: Friends of our forests. *Natl. Geogr*. 63 (4): 453–79.

Phillips, A. R., J. Marshall, and G. Monson. 1964. *The Birds of Arizona*. Tucson: University of Arizona Press.

Phillips, J. C. 1926. An attempt to list the extinct and vanishing birds of the Western Hemisphere. In *Proceedings of the Sixth International Ornithological Congress*, 512–13. Copenhagen, Denmark.

Pindar, L. O. 1889. Birds of Fulton County, Kentucky. *Auk* 6: 310–16.

Plimpton, G. 1977. Un gran pedazo de carne. *Audubon* 79 (6): 10–25.

Remsen, J. V. 1995. The importance of continued collecting of bird specimens to ornithology and bird conservation. *Bird Conservation International* 5: 145–80.

Ridgway, R. R. 1887. The imperial woodpecker (*Campephilus imperialis*) in northern Sonora. *Auk* 4: 161.

———. 1900. *A manual of North American birds*. 4th ed. Philadelphia: Lippincott.

Robinson, W. D., J. D. Brawn, and S. K. Robinson. 2000. Forest bird community structure in central Panama: Influence of spatial scale and biogeography. *Ecol. Monogr*. 70 (2): 209–35.

Romney, T. C. 1938. *Mormons in Mexico*. Salt Lake City, UT: Deseret Book.

Rozzi, D., D. Martinez, M. F. Wilson, and C. Sabag. 1996. Avifauna de los bosques templados de Sudamerica. In *Ecologica de los bosques nativos de Chile*, ed. J. Armesto, D. Villagrán, and M. Kalin Arroyo, 135–52. Santiago: Editorial Universitaria, Univ. de Chile.

Rumiz, D. I., D. Guinart S., L. Solar R., and J. C. Herrera. 2001. Logging and hunting in community forests and corporate concessions. In *The cutting edge: Conserving wildlife in logged tropical forest*, ed. R. A. Fimbel, A. Grajal, and J. Robinson, 333–57. New York: Columbia University Press.

Russell, S. R., and G. Monson. 1998. *The birds of Sonora*. Tucson: University of Arizona Press.

Salvin, O., and F. D. Godman. 1888–97. *Biologia Centrali-Americana*. Vol. 2 of *Aves*. London: privately published.

Sauer, G. C. 1998. *John Gould the bird man: Correspondence*. Vol. 1. Mansfield Centre, CT: Maurizio Martino.

Schardien, B. J., and J. A. Jackson. 1978. Extensive ground foraging by pileated woodpeckers in recently burned pine forests. *Mississippi Kite* 8: 7–9.

Schlatter, R. P., and P. Vergara. 2005. Magellanic woodpecker (*Campephilus magellanicus*) sap feeding and its role in the Tierra del Fuego forest bird assemblage. *J. Ornithol* 146: 188–90.

Sclater, P. L., and O. Salvin. 1859. On the ornithology of Central America, Part 2. *Ibis* 1: 117–38.

Scott, W. E. D. 1888. Supplementary notes from the Gulf Coast of Florida, with a description of a new species of Marsh Wren. *Auk* 5: 183–88.

———. 1898. *Bird studies.* New York: Putnam's Sons.

———. 1903. *The story of a bird lover.* New York: MacMillan.

Selander, R. K. 1966. Sexual dimorphism and differential niche utilization in birds. *Condor* 68: 113–51.

Sheldon, C. 1979. The big game of Chihuahua, Mexico, 1898–1902. In *The wilderness of desert bighorns and Seri Indians*, ed. D. E. Brown, N. B. Carmony, and P. M. Webb, 144–68. Phoenix: Arizona Desert Bighorn Sheep Society.

Short, L. L. 1970. The habits and relationships of the Magellanic woodpecker. *Wilson Bull.* 82: 115–29.

———. 1982. *Woodpeckers of the world.* Monograph series 4. Greenville: Delaware Museum of Natural History.

Short, L. L., and J. F. M. Horne. 1986. The ivorybill still lives. *Nat. Hist.* 95 (7): 26–28.

———. 1987. I saw it! *Int. Wildl.* 17 (2): 22–23.

———. 1990. The ivory-billed woodpecker: The costs of specialization. In *Conservation and management of woodpecker populations*, ed. A Carlson and G. Aulen, 93–98. Report 17. Uppsala: Swedish University of Agricultural Sciences, Department of Wildlife Ecology.

Sibley, D. A., L. R. Bevier, M. A. Patten, and C. S. Elphick. 2006. Comment on "Ivory-billed woodpecker (*Campephilus principalis*) persists in continental North America." *Science* 311: 1555.

Skutch, A. F. 1969. *Life histories of Central American birds III.* Pacific Coast Avifauna. Monograph no. 35. Berkeley: Cooper Ornithological Society.

Slud, P. 1964. The birds of Costa Rica: Distribution and ecology. *Bull. Amer. Mus. Nat. Hist.* 128: 189.

Smith, A. P. 1908. Destruction of imperial woodpeckers. *Condor* 10: 91.

Smith, W. 1952. *Kiva mural decorations at Awatovi an Kawaika-a, with a survey of other wall paintings in the Pueblo Southwest.* Vol. 37 of *American archeology and ethnology papers.* Cambridge, MA: Harvard University, Peabody Museum.

Snyder, N., and H. A. Snyder. 2000. *The California condor: A saga of natural history and conservation.* London: Academic.

———. 2005. *Introduction to the California condor.* Berkeley: University of California Press.

———. 2006. *Raptors of North America, natural history and conservation.* St. Paul, MN: Voyageur.

Snyder, N. F. R. 2004. *The Carolina parakeet: Glimpses of a vanished bird.* Princeton, NJ: Princeton University Press.

———. 2007. *An alternative hypothesis for the cause of the ivory-billed woodpecker's decline.* Monographs of the Western Foundation of Vertebrate Zoology 2.

Snyder, N. F. R., S. R. Derrickson, S. R. Beissinger, J. W. Wiley, T. B. Smith, W. D. Toone, and B. Miller. 1996. Limitations of captive breeding in endangered species recovery. *Conserv. Biol.* 10: 338–48.

Snyder, N. F. R., E. C. Enkerlin-Hoeflich, and M. A. Cruz-Nieto. 1999. Thick-billed parrot (*Rhynchopsitta pachyrhyncha*). In *The birds of North America*, ed. A. Poole and F. Gill. Monograph no. 406. Philadelphia: Birds of North America.

Sonnichsen, C. L. 1974. *Colonel Greene and the copper skyrocket*. Tucson: University of Arizona Press.

Steinberg, M. K. 2008. *Stalking the ghost bird*. Baton Rouge: Louisiana State University Press.

Steinhart, P. 1999. A common possession. In *The National Audubon Society: Speaking for nature, a century of conservation*, ed. L. Line, 42–59. New York: Hugh Lauter Levin Associates.

Stoddard, H. L. 1951. Unpublished letter to John Baker. National Audubon Society archives, Tavernier, Florida.

———. 1969. *Memoirs of a naturalist*. Norman: University of Oklahoma Press.

Stokstad, E. 2007. Gambling on a ghost bird. *Science* 317: 888–92.

Swarth, H. S. 1929. *The C.O.C. 1893–1928*. San Francisco: Cooper Ornithological Club.

Tanner, J. T. 1935–40. Unpublished field notes. Ithaca, NY: Cornell University libraries.

———. 1940. The life history and ecology of the ivory-billed woodpecker. PhD diss., Cornell University, Ithaca, New York.

———. 1941. Three years with the ivory-billed woodpecker, America's rarest bird. *Audubon Magazine* 43: 4–14.

———. 1942. *The ivory-billed woodpecker*. Research report 1. New York: National Audubon Society.

———. 1964. The decline and present status of the imperial woodpecker of Mexico. *Auk* 81: 74–81.

Taylor, R. V., and S. K. Albert. 1999. Human hunting of nongame birds at Zuni, New Mexico, USA. *Conserv. Biol.* 13 (6): 1398–403.

Terborgh, J., S. K. Robinson, T. A. Parker III, C. A. Munn, and N. Pierpont. 1990. Structure and organization of an Amazonian forest bird community. *Ecol. Monogr.* 60: 213–38.

Thayer, J. E. 1906. Eggs and nest of the thick-billed parrot. *Auk* 23: 223–24.

Thayer, J. E., and O. Bangs. 1908. The present state of the ornis of Guadaloupe Island. *Condor* 10 (3): 101–6.

Thiollay, J.-M. 1994. Structure, density, and rarity in an Amazonian rainforest bird community. *J. Trop. Ecol.* 10: 449–81.

Thompson, M. 1889. A red-headed family. *Oologist* 6 (2): 23–29.

Tinker, B. 1978. *Mexican wilderness and wildlife*. Austin: University of Texas Press.

Uranga-Thomas, R., and D. Venegas-Holguin. 1995. Determination of the existence of the imperial woodpecker in the state of Chihuahua, Mexico. Unpubl. ms. submitted to U.S. Fish and Wildlife Service. Chihuahua, Mexico: Fundación Chihuahuense de la Fauna, A.C.

U.S. Congress. 1973. *The Endangered Species Act*. P.L. 93-205 and P.L. 94-325, as amended. Washington, DC: Government Printing Office.

USFWS. 2005. *Cache River National Wildlife Refuge public use, hunting and fishing regulations 2005–2006*. Augusta, AR: U.S. Fish and Wildlife Service.

———. 2006. *Recovery plan for the ivory-billed woodpecker (Campephilus principalis)*. Atlanta, GA: U.S. Fish and Wildlife Service.

van Riper, C., III, and J. M. Scott. 2001. Limiting factors affecting Hawaiian native birds. In *Evolution, ecology, conservation, and management of Hawaiian birds: A vanishing avifauna*, ed. J. M. Scott, S. Conant, and C. van Riper III,

221–33. Studies in Avian Biology. Monograph no. 22. Cooper Ornithological Society

van Riper, C., III, S. G. van Riper, M. L. Goff, and M. Laird. 1986. The epizootiology and ecological significance of malaria in Hawaiian land birds. *Ecol. Monogr.* 56: 327–44.

van Riper, C., III, S. G. van Riper, and W. R. Hansen. 2002. Epizootiology and effect of avian pox on Hawaiian forest birds. *Auk* 119: 929–42.

van Rossem, A. J. 1945. A distributional survey of the birds of Sonora, Mexico. *Occas. Papers Mus. Zool., Louisiana State Univ.* Monograph no. 21.

Vasquez, M. 1996. *¿Montañas, duendes, advinos?* Mexico City: México Instituto Nacional Indigenistas.

Warner, R. E. 1968. The role of introduced diseases in the extinction of the endemic Hawaiian avifauna. *Condor* 70: 101–20.

Wayne, A. T. 1893. Additional notes on the birds of the Suwanee River. *Auk* 10: 336–38.

———. 1895. Notes on the birds of the Wacissa and Aucilla River regions of Florida. *Auk* 12: 362–67.

Wiedensaul, S. 2005. The ivory-bill and its forest breathe new life. *Nature Conservancy* 55 (2): 20–31.

Wilkie, D. S., J. G. Sidle, G. C. Boundzanga, P. Auzel, and S. Blake. 2001. Defaunation, not deforestation, commercial logging and market hunting in northern Congo. In *The cutting edge, conserving wildlife in logged tropical forest*, ed. R. A. Fimbel, A. Grajal, and J. Robinson, 375–99. New York: Columbia University Press.

Williams, B. F. 1984. *Let the tail go with the hide.* El Paso, TX: Mangan Books.

Williams, R. W. 1904. Preliminary list of the birds of Leon County, Florida. *Auk* 21 (4): 449–62.

Wilson, A. 1811. *American ornithology.* Vol. 4. Philadelphia: Bradford and Inskeep.

Winkler, H., D. A. Christie, and D. Nurney. 1995. *Woodpeckers: A guide to the woodpeckers of the world.* Boston: Houghton Mifflin.

Wood, L. 1970. *Chasing Geronimo: The journal of Leonard Wood, May–September 1886.* Albuquerque: University of New Mexico Press.

INDEX

ivory-bill distribution in, 3 map 1; ivory-bill observations in, 26; ivory-bill occurrence in, 20, 22, 23 table 1, 24, 135–37; ivory-bill rediscovery in, 2–3, 6, 117; last ivory-bills in, 14; remnant ivory-bill populations in, 14, 16–17
Fort Drum Swamp, 20, plates 5 and 6
Franklin Parish, La., 54
Frazer, M. A., 75

Goldman, E. A., 71, 73, 99
González, Guillermo Carillo, plate 21, 96–97, 108
González-Romero, Alberto, 89, 96
Gould, John, 68–69, 140–41, 151
Graves, Gary, 113–14
great auk, 117, 132, 133
great slaty woodpecker, 1, 91
Griscom, Ludlow, 128
grizzly bear, 104, 123, 132, 133

habitat: conservation of, 115–17; degradation or loss of, 7, 8, 12, 110, 112, 121, 131–34; preservation of, 131–34. *See also under* Cuban Ivory-billed woodpecker; imperial woodpecker; ivory-billed woodpecker
hackberry, ivory-bill damaged, 34
Hankins, Dr. E. A., III, 4, plate 17, 86–88
Hasbrouck, Edwin, 14, 21, 22, 30, 53, 55
Howard, Bob, 88–89, 140, plate 18
Huichol Indians, plate 11, 68, 96–97
human depredation: protection from, 133. *See also under* Cuban ivory-billed woodpecker; imperial woodpecker; ivory-billed woodpecker
hunting, regulation of, 117, 118, 119, 131. *See also under* imperial woodpecker; ivory-billed woodpecker

Imperial woodpecker, plates 10 and 12; acorn stealing of, 91, 101; approachability of, 8–9, 104, 111; beak of, plates 13 and 22, 68, 91; behavior of, 7, 73, 100–101, 103; breeding sites of, 92, 93; call of, 9, 73, 74, 83, 84, 87, 103; collecting of, 68, 69, 71, 73, 75–79, 99, 102, 103, 104; coloration of, 1–2; comparisons

of ivory-bill with, plate 22, 62–63, 84; conservation of, 112, 114, 116, 126; crest of, 2, plates 10 and 13, 68, 75, 92, 94, 100; decline of, 1, 7–9, 92, 102–5, 109–14; density of, 93, 101–2, 110; depictions of, plate 24, 106, 107; description of, plates 13 and 22, 68, 73, 74–75, 79; diet of, plate 27, 82, 101, 106–7, 111; dispersal of, 105; display mounts of, plates 14 and 18, 72, 79, 88–89; distribution of, 68–69, 98–99, 105–8; early accounts of, 67, 70–77, 99, 101, 103, 110–11, 127; edibility of, 111; eggs of, 4, 67, 73, 75, 100; evidence of, 1, 4, 81–82, 85, 88, 92, 94, 120; exploitation of, 106; extirpation of, 51, 110; feathers of, 1, 86, 92; feeding habits of, 10, 73, 84, 101, 109, 119; fledglings of, 83, 100; flight of, 73, 84; food source of, 82; as food specialist, 107–8, 109–11; food supply of, 102, 106–8, 110–12, 114; foraging techniques of, 111; habitat of, plates 15 and 19, 69, 73, 93, 96–97, 98–99, 102, 103–4, 105; habitat loss, 62, 84, 86, 89, 93, 97; habitat survey, 91; human depredation of, xi, 7–9, 102, 111–12, 114–23; hunting of, 89, 91, 92, 103, 104, 110, 123; interviews on, 10, 82–83, 86, 89, 90–91, 92; killing of, 8, 12, 70, 83, 84, 86, 92, 123, 138–53; last verifiable account of, 81; medicinal value of, 71, 92, 103, 104; monogamy by, 99; museum collections of, 67, 68, 69, 70, 73, 76, 79, 97, 102, 138–53; natural history of, 4, 70, 71, 73, 82, 91, 98–102, 103; nesting cavities of, plate 17, 81, 82, 84, 87–88, 90; nests of, 4 , 71, 82, 100; petroglyph of, plate 24; photographic evidence of, 4, plate 10, 67, 85; population density of, 101–2, 110–11, 112; range of, 4, 5 map 2, 6, 10, 68–69, 104–8; recovery of, 119, 120–25; remnant populations of, 7, 73, 89, 114, 119, 120–25, 129; reproductive rate of, 9, 99; roosting cavities of, 73, 81, 84; scarcity of, 70–71, 104; sedentary behavior of, 105; sex ratios of, 99; shooting of, 8, 51, 71, 78, 79, 84, 85, 89, 93, 111, 114–15, 117, 119–21; sightings of, 4, 6, plate 10, 70, 79,